# REINCARNATION

Stories *of* Mercy & Resolution

Other titles by Elizabeth Clare Prophet

*Reincarnation: The Missing Link in Christianity*

*Karma and Reincarnation*

*The Afterlife*

*The Lost Years of Jesus*

*The Opening of the Seventh Seal*

# REINCARNATION

## Stories *of* Mercy & Resolution

Karmic Revelations
*of* Eight Influential People

*with*

Elizabeth Clare Prophet

Summit University Press®
Gardiner, Montana

Reincarnation Stories of Mercy and Resolution
*Karmic Revelations of Eight Influential People*
by Elizabeth Clare Prophet


Previously published as *9 Cats, 9 Lives: Influential People and Their Past Lives.*



For information, contact
The Summit Lighthouse, 63 Summit Way, Gardiner, MT 59030 USA
Tel: 1-800-245-5445 or 1 406-848-9500
TSLinfo@TSL.org
SummitLighthouse.org



Library of Congress Control Number: 2024936814
ISBN: 978-1-60988-484-0 (softbound)
ISBN: 978-1-60988-485-7 (eBook)

SUMMIT UNIVERSITY PRESS®



27 26 25 24 1 2 3 4

# Contents


Introduction . . . . . . . . . . . . . . . . . vii

1 Karma and Reincarnation . . . . . . . 1

2 Nine Lives of Henry Ford . . . . . . . . 19

3 Nine Lives and Another Chance . . . . 39

4 The Diaries of a Narcissist . . . . . . . 65

5 The Use and Misuse of Power . . . . . 81

6 Tests Passed and Karma Balanced . . . 91

7 The Iron Lady . . . . . . . . . . . . . 101

8 Charles Lindbergh . . . . . . . . . . . 109

9 Babe Ruth . . . . . . . . . . . . . . . 143

10 Elizabeth Clare Prophet . . . . . . . . 155

11 Where Do We Go from Here? . . . . . 183

12 The Violet Flame . . . . . . . . . . . 197

Discussion Questions . . . . . . . . . . . 205

Notes . . . . . . . . . . . . . . . . . . . 207

# Introduction

I believe that karma and reincarnation are the most important concepts that we can understand to discover the meaning of life, to answer imponderable questions, to understand our reason for being.

God revealed the concept of reincarnation to me at a very early age. But I am not unique in this. Many people have had the experience of remembering a past life in some way. Before we're through, some of you who think you haven't remembered a past life may realize that you have.

We've all had the sense of being familiar with a person or place that we've never contacted before in this life—kind of an instantaneous like or dislike. Even love at first sight signifies an inner soul knowing.

We have little hints but, as a matter of fact, there is a reason why we specifically don't remember our past. God in his mercy pulls the shade when we enter the birth canal. It's a "curtain of forgetfulness." This is an act of mercy because we have an assignment for this life and we can't really focus on more than one life at a time and make a go of it.

But now and then God raises the shade and shows us a frame or two from a previous life episode. This is for the quickening of our souls as to our responsibilities in this life and the commitments we made before coming into embodiment this time around. God sends his angels to teach us from the record of our own karmic book of life so that we can make enlightened choices and pass our tests.

Because even now at inner levels God is teaching your soul about your karma and your past incarnations, I am going to tell you how I first learned about karma and reincarnation in the hope that my story will ring a bell for you. What I'm about to tell you is the first time I recall God raising the shade for me.

One day when I was about four years old, I was playing in my sandbox in Red Bank, New Jersey, where I was born. I was in the play yard that my father had made for me. It had a playhouse, a swing and sandbox enclosed by a white picket fence with an arch and gate. It was situated next to a delightful garden created by my parents.

It was a beautiful day. Big white clouds were moving through a deep blue sky. And I was alone, enjoying myself in the sun, watching the sand slip through my little fingers, drawing designs in the fresh earth and making mudpies with cookie cutters and tin molds.

Then all of a sudden, as though someone had turned a dial, I was playing in the sand along the Nile River in Egypt and I was experiencing the beauty of that scene. It was just as real as my play yard in Red Bank and just as familiar. I was idling away the hours, splashing in the water and feeling the warm sand on my body. My Egyptian mother was nearby. Somehow this, too, was my world. I had known that river forever.

After some time (I don't know how much time had passed), it was as though the dial turned again and I was back at home in that little play yard. I wasn't dizzy. I wasn't dazed. I was back to the present, very much aware that I had been somewhere else.

So I jumped up and ran to find my mother. I found her at the kitchen stove and I blurted out my story. I said, "Mother, what happened?" She sat me down and looked at me and said, "You have remembered a past life." With those words she opened another dimension. And I have never been the same.

Instead of ridiculing or denying what I had experienced, she explained that the soul does not accomplish her mission in one life. She told me that my soul was eternal. She said that our body is like a coat we wear: it gets worn out before we finish what we have to do. So God gives us a new mommy and a new daddy and we are born again so we can finish the work God sent us to do and finally return to our home of light in heaven. Even though we get a new body, we are still the same soul. And the soul has a continuous recollection of the past, but we do not.

She explained all of this to me in simple childlike terms I understood. It was as though I had always known it and my mother was reawakening my soul memory.

Over the years she was to point out to me children who were born maimed or blind, others who were gifted, some who were born into wealthy homes and some into poverty. She attributed their inequality to karma and to their past exercise of free will. She said that there could be no such thing as divine or human justice if we had only one life, that God's justice could only be known in the outplaying of many lives in which we see past actions coming full circle in present circumstances.

Accustomed to praying to Jesus, my thoughts turned to him. I saw the logic of reincarnation and I said to myself, "God must have shown me this past life for a reason." But God didn't tell me the reason till I was well into adulthood. Then I realized that that life in Egypt was the key to the work I had to do in this life. No doubt, through that glimpse into the distant past, there was transferred to me some substance of myself—perhaps some heavy karma that I had to balance today, thirty-three centuries later, or a mission I had not fulfilled whose time had come.

Since then God has revealed to me other incarnations and

taught me lessons concerning positive or negative momentums that I must build on or undo. Thus, I have seen the causes behind the effects of bad karma that I had to balance in this life, and I have seen how my good karma put the wind in my sails to achieve my goals and more. Karma, in fact, is why we are all here.

You, too, have brought with you the momentums of your good karma as well as those of your bad karma that you must balance. You most certainly have positive or negative karma with family members and people you know or people you will meet. Life is a challenge and an opportunity.

Some people dismiss the belief in reincarnation as wishful thinking or escapism. It can become that for some. But for others, it can be a powerful tool for spiritual development. Reincarnation tells us that life is a continuum. It tells us that what we did in our past lives affects our current life. Understanding this can help us to overcome phobias, chronic health problems, difficulties in relationships and even personality traits that undermine us in our career.

Scientists say that they do not know how to measure or study reincarnation—how do you put a trace on a soul? Nevertheless, a growing number of doctors and scientists are becoming convinced that there is something—a higher intelligence, a spiritual energy—that directs affairs in the body and disengages from it upon death. It may be that scientists will one day be able to measure and track the path of this energy—call it soul or consciousness if you will—from one body to the next.

In the meantime, let us explore the ramifications of reincarnation and what difference it can make to our ideas about life today. It is part of a belief system that answers many of the questions we are asking ourselves: Why am I here? Why did I get the parents that I got? Why am I afraid of airplanes? Why do I like banana splits? What do I want to do with my life?

CHAPTER 1

# Karma and Reincarnation

The belief in reincarnation is ancient and widespread. We find it not only in the Orient—India, China, and Japan—but also in pre-Christian Europe. Before the advent of Christianity, reincarnation was a part of the spiritual beliefs of many of the peoples of Europe, including the early Teutonic tribes, the Finns, Icelanders, Lapps, Norwegians, Swedes, Danes, early Saxons and the Celts of Ireland, Scotland, England, Brittany, Gaul and Wales. The Welsh have even claimed that it was the Celts who originally carried the belief of reincarnation to India.[1] Author Ignatius Donnelly suggests that the Celts' belief in reincarnation was derived from inhabitants of the lost continent of Atlantis who migrated to Ireland.[2]

In ancient Greece, both Pythagoras and Plato believed in reincarnation. In the sixth century BC, Pythagoras taught that the soul has had many incarnations, which were opportunities for the soul to purify and perfect herself. "The human soul is immortal," he said, "for it resembles the heavenly stars, and (like them) is involved in perpetual motion."[3]

According to biographer Diogenes Laertius, Pythagoras claimed that he had been embodied in the past as Aethalides and as Euphorbus, who died at the hands of Menelaus at Troy.[4]

According to some scholars, statements made by the first-century Jewish historian Josephus indicate that the Pharisees and Essenes also believed in reincarnation. Others believe these are references to the resurrection of the dead in new bodies.[5]

Reincarnation was also taught by students of the Kabbalah, a system of Jewish esoteric mysticism that flowered in the thirteenth century. Reincarnation is still a part of the religious beliefs of the Jewish Hasidic movement, which was founded in the eighteenth century.

Some tribes of American Indians as well as numerous tribes in Central and South America have believed in reincarnation. Today the belief in reincarnation also exists among over one hundred tribes in Africa as well as among Eskimo and Central Australian tribes and many peoples of the Pacific, including Hawaiians, Tahitians, Melanesians and Okinawans.

The most elaborately developed concepts of reincarnation are found in the religious traditions of India, especially Hinduism, Buddhism, Jainism and Sikhism. In these religions, reincarnation is linked with the law of karma.

## The Law of Karma

*Karma* is a Sanskrit word meaning "act, action, work or deed." In Hinduism *karma* originally referred to sacred actions performed in Vedic rituals and later evolved to mean moral codes and moral deeds. It then became associated with the concept of reincarnation in another body or form of life.

According to the law of karma as it is taught in the East, your thoughts, your words and deeds in past lives have determined the conditions of your present life; and your thoughts, words and deeds in this life will determine your destiny in future lives.

This is a bit difficult for most Westerners to accept. People like to blame their parents or circumstances or heredity or what happened to them when they were children or the opportunities they've missed—everything but themselves. I think that the Church's doctrine of the vicarious atonement (that Jesus Christ paid the debt for our sins) perpetuates our sense of wanting someone else to carry the burden of our karma, in other words, the burden of our sin.

This is reflected in the credit system we have in this nation. We can get anything on credit—just take out your card and charge it. As a result of this system, many middle-class Americans have gone bankrupt, and this shows a moral bankruptcy as well as a financial bankruptcy. It is a philosophy of not paying as you go and not being responsible for your actions.

If some calamity happens to us, we think, "Well, this is so-and-so's fault." Or "I was a victim of circumstances." "I was at the wrong place at the wrong time." Some people blame God for what happens to them and stay angry at him for the rest of their lives and even for embodiments to come. These attitudes are wrong. We have to get into the driver's seat and take responsibility for our lives and our actions.

I myself have certainly not had an easy life. I recall petitioning the Lords of Karma before I took embodiment to allow me to take on a major portion of my karma at birth, and they did. And I accept that most of the things that have happened to me, good or bad, have come about by my own doings.

I say "most" because people initiate original acts of negative karma every day. People willfully harm people, just as nation inflicts harm upon nation where there is no antecedent of a prior karma between them. Thus the injured party is not the recipient of returning karma of the past, but the victim of an initial act of wrongdoing. This is why we can truthfully say that not everything that happens to us is the result of our own doings.

Then there is the situation of the initiation of our souls. This comes from the Universal Christ. And there is temptation. This comes from the Antichrist. Initiation and temptation are the means God allows for the testing of our souls. The story of Job is a classic example of calamity which God allows so that our love for him can be tested. These trials teach us lessons. When we pass through them without compromising our honor, we are ready for the next trial and the next until we graduate from earth's schoolroom.

So our good karma brings untold blessings as the harvest of our good works. Our bad karma brings the harvest of what we have sown in error. And we do not escape one jot or one tittle of it.[6] But it is true that we may receive good or bad energy from others, neither of which we deserve. Every day people exercise their free will to be kind or unkind—regardless of past karma. They are making new karma and they will receive blessing or bane accordingly, just as we do when we initiate actions that are wise or unwise.

Initiations, including persecution and the crucifixion, are sent by God to strengthen us and restore our souls back to him. Temptation is a testing of the mettle of the soul. Since we cannot always tell whether the good fortune that befalls us is due to our good karma or the sheer mercy and grace of God, and we do not know if adversity is our bad karma coming back to haunt us or temptation or trial or soul testing or the highest levels of initiation from God, we must therefore deal with every circumstance with a positive, grateful attitude. We must determine that we will deal justly with ourselves, our God and our fellowman so that there will be a victory, a blessing and a resolution for all concerned.

So you see there are circumstances in our lives that cannot be classified strictly as karma—except it be our karmic lot to endure all things because it is we who left off from the presence of God in the first place. And now we have the karma of finding our way back to him "by the sweat of the brow" until our original sin of turning away from God is balanced.

In my sense, then, of God and the universe, I have only gratitude for the lessons I have learned from my karma. For I understood the law of karma in my heart before it was ever taught to me. My motto is: There is no injustice anywhere in the universe. Amazing as it may seem, if we knew *all* the circumstances and ramifications of our past lives, our past "rights" and "wrongs," we would see clearly that this is true.

If we understood the continuity of being and all that we have said and done in past ages, we would see that our words and deeds return to us as our teachers. And if they are not-so-nice, we should understand that not-so-nice things happen to us so that we can self-correct. They happen so that we can see how it feels to be on the receiving end of what we have sent forth in this or a previous lifetime.

I think it is the coming of age of a man, a woman or a child when the soul reaches that point of maturity where she can say, "Whatever comes to me, I will receive it with rejoicing. For I know that as I balance and resolve that situation, I can look forward to my communion with God and ultimately to that day when I can attain permanent reunion with my Divine Father and my Divine Mother."

Hinduism and Buddhism teach that the law of karma is a universal law of cause and effect that affects everyone. As Newton's third law of motion states: For every action there is an equal and opposite reaction. In the same way as the laws of physics, the law of karma operates automatically and without prejudice. This is why justice prevails. This is why there is hope for each one of us.

We think that some people get away with everything while we get away with nothing. We simply have to be at peace and remember the teaching from Deuteronomy which Paul quoted: "Vengeance is mine. I will repay, saith the Lord."[7] Therefore it is ours to forgive. God will mete out his justice and we certainly do not wish harm upon anyone, even those who are our self-styled enemies.

Karma functions on an individual as well as on a group level. As the twentieth-century Hindu yogi Yogananda wrote: "The cumulative actions of human beings within communities, nations or the world as a whole constitutes mass karma, which produces local or far-ranging effects according to the degree and preponderance of good or evil. The thoughts and actions of every man, therefore, contribute to the good or ill of this world and all peoples in it."[8]

There is, then, such a thing as personal karma, something very personal, for instance, between you and me alone; it functions one on one. And then there is group karma. Entire nations or towns or families have made karma because of their stand against life. They commit acts together as one body and therefore they must reembody together. The Mafia families, for instance, come back together again and again because of their karma—made amongst themselves and with their victims outside of the mob.

According to Eastern teachings, karma necessitates rebirth because you can't reap all the effects of your karma in a single lifetime. This is true. There is simply not enough time in one lifetime to experience the return of, or the compensation for, all the good or the bad you have done in that life. Therefore we must come back multiple times. And these times stretch out into ages because we must reembody at the same time as others with whom we have karma to balance or a mission or a project to complete. It may take many cycles and many centuries before the stage is set once again for us to be with the same group of people that we were with where we made our karma, good or bad, in the first place.

## Karma and Free Will

There is a misunderstanding among some in the West that the Eastern concept of karma is fatalistic. People sometimes say to me: "Oh, you believe in karma and reincarnation. You'll be taking another million years before you get to God!"

That's not my concept of karma. I also believe in grace. I believe in the grace of my Lord and Saviour Jesus Christ and I believe in that Christ, that only begotten Son of God, that is apportioned to each one of us. With the help of the Mediator, the Universal One and the very personal one in Jesus and the one whom God gave to me and to you, I trust that I shall and will balance my karma in this life and I trust that you will, also.

Some people think that Hindus believe there's no way out of your karma, that you'll be embodying here for so long that it might as well be forever, which almost renders the concept of karma null and void—it is so long in returning that it is almost never, so you start not worrying about karma at all. But that is really not today's teaching of Hinduism or Buddhism.

The Hindu teaching on karma, as described in the *Ramakrishna-Vedanta Wordbook,* is that "the fruits of karma are reaped in the form of happiness or misery, according to the nature of each thought or act. Although each person imposes upon himself the limitation of his own character as determined by his past thoughts and actions, at the same time he has a choice. Devotion to God, enhancing good karmas and mitigating evil ones, begins to loosen the bonds of karma. When a man achieves illumination, his acts cease to produce karmas."[9]

This is what Saint Germain and other ascended masters have been telling us for years. So many of us are the victims of predestination, of a fatalistic type of consciousness—"what will be, will be, and we have nothing to say about it." Free will comes from the divine spark. It comes from the presence of Christ, or the Light within us. *Christ* is not necessarily a Christian term. It comes from the Greek word *christos,* which means "anointed." So the Christ is the anointed one, the Real Self of each of us.

By that presence of God with us, we understand that every single day and moment we exercise free will. We make a decision to be constructive or destructive or somewhere in between. Of course, there is no neutrality in life, so we had better decide which side we're on and take a strong stand for that side.

Free will is the means whereby we make good karma or negative karma. Free will is the pivot of existence and true being. Free will makes us sons and daughters of God instead of mechanization man—automatons or robots created by Atlantean or present-day scientists. We have to understand that free will is our capacity to become the full manifestation of God when we have our victory.

We have a choice as to what we will do when karma descends. We can either follow the tendency of our karma and our past, which is written also in our astrology, or we can challenge it. We can struggle against it. We can say, "I am not the victim of my stars or my fate or my past karma. I am a new being. I am a new creature in Christ. And this day I determine that I will be all-love in action. And if I hated my neighbor yesterday, I will love my neighbor today. That is my free will. And I summon the will of God to assist me to change my course, the set of my sails, toward the mark of victory in this life."

You have the freedom to do this today. You can make your decision. You can make a vow to God to be who you really are and to fulfill your destiny.

Free will allows us to look at a terrible karma that has descended upon us and decide how we will respond to it. We wake up one morning and find that our wife has left with our children, our husband has disappeared, our house has burned down or our business is destroyed. Calamities come upon people.

But because we have free will we can say: "I will not be moved by this karma! I understand it as a blessing and as a teaching and I will take my lessons from it. I will overcome it. I will get beyond it. I will contact my God. I will cry out to my God, as the psalmist did, and he will hear me. He will not fail me now." It's not what happens to us in life, it's how we react to it that makes all the difference.

## Karma in the Old Testament

The law of cause and effect, which is the law of karma, is firmly rooted in the Judeo-Christian tradition. Most people do not realize this—simply because the preachers do not preach it from the pulpits. But the Old Testament is filled with stories of the hammer of karmic law exacting penalties for bad actions and rewards for good actions.

You can't miss karma in the Old Testament, starting with the sinking of Atlantis, which is called the Flood of Noah. The karma of Atlantis descended for the misuse of God's sacred fire in all of the chakras, for the genetic engineering of creatures that were half human and half animal,[10] for the misqualification of science and the light on the altar of the temple.

This karma descended horrendously. The entire continent sank for that karma. And it was coming for thousands upon thousands of years. The people had warnings. They knew it was coming but they did not change their ways. Prophets and great teachers came into their cities and spoke to them. But the people would not abandon their rebellion against God and embrace him and his laws.

After that flood, the Bible records that God enjoined Noah and his sons, "Whoso sheddeth man's blood, by man shall his blood be shed: for in the image of God made he man."[11]

Some Bible commentators, including Scofield, say that this statement shows the beginning of the institution of human government for the protection of human life. It also states the law of karma. Jesus said the same thing: "He that taketh the sword shall fall by the sword."[12]

In Exodus, God details the law-code for Israel, which includes the command: "He that smiteth a man so that he die shall be surely put to death.... If any mischief follow, then thou shalt give life for life, eye for eye, tooth for tooth, hand for hand, foot for foot, burning for burning, wound for wound, stripe for stripe."[13] This shows that the law of karma was codified in the laws of the nations to protect human life.

Both the Old and New Testaments show the doings of a people whom God loves and wants to bring back to himself. The Hebrew people are not the unique chosen people—all people may choose and therefore be chosen to embrace God and his laws and to return to his heart. People learn that disobedience to God's law brings about an untimely passing and the necessity to reembody again. That is the case in the Old Testament. By and by, after numerous incarnations, they begin to fear the Law and finally they love it.

Without reincarnation, it is impossible to understand why God would allow or bring about the death of so many people for seemingly not-so-bad crimes. We don't see our deeds from past lives, whose karma is coming due. But if we could see what is written in our karmic book of life by recording angels, we would realize that the karma of five, ten or twelve thousand years could descend upon any of us at any time. Yes, if we could see all of this, we would exclaim with the angel: "Even so, Lord God Almighty, true and righteous are thy judgments!"[14]

When we understand karma and reincarnation, we see that God's priority for us is not success, money and pleasure. God's priority for us is that we get our souls back into alignment with him.

## Karma in the New Testament

Jesus affirmed the law of karma and reincarnation that is taught in the Old Testament. In his Sermon on the Mount, he says: "Think not that I am come to destroy the law or the prophets: I am not come to destroy but to fulfill."[15] So Jesus came to fulfill the law that is written in the Old Testament and the prophets who proclaimed it. And truly this law was the law of karma.

Think of your actions as your karma that you are making right now, positive karma because your actions are constructive, or negative because they are less than constructive. It is as simple as that.

What you do and say and how you spend your time, all of this is how you are using God's energy and impressing upon the aura of your town and your city good energies, high energies, or low ones. If you are depressed, you are affecting other people with your depression, and you are responsible for that. Your depression or your anger can go out for miles—and so can your love or your joy or your singing or your happiness or your prayers. Everything you do is multiplied, affecting many.

So take accountability for your thoughts and feelings and actions. Get on the right side of the law of karma and it will be wind in your sails. The law of karma will work for you, and it will multiply and increase your blessings day upon day.

Jesus sets forth a law that will not be broken. These are not the words of the Old Testament prophets and patriarchs. These are the words of our Lord: "But I say unto you, that every idle word that men shall speak, they shall give account thereof in the day of judgment. For by thy words thou shalt be justified, and by thy words thou shalt be condemned."[16] The word *condemned* here means "judged." Jesus is telling us the consequences of every idle word, every unkind word, every juicy piece of gossip, everything that we say that is excessive and nonessential and does not contribute to everlasting life or the good of the community in which we live.

Words are power. Where do we get the power to speak? We get it from God, from our I AM Presence. Let us give reverence to that power and use it to spread peace and comfort, to stop arguments, to help people love one another. Let us get beyond the pettiness of life and realize that if we are petty, the karma of pettiness will return to us. And if we are magnanimous, that good karma will return also.

If we are accountable for every idle word that we speak, how much are we accountable for every act—as well as the state of mind or mindlessness that precedes the act or the desire that impels it? The law of karma gives us sound reason to control our tongues as well as the uncontrolled thoughts and feelings that propel our tongues.

If we know that we're likely to have an accident when we drink and drive, and in spite of this we take people out in a car and they are killed, our karma began when we took that drink. If we know we're going to be absolutely mindless under the influence of drugs and we take those drugs, we are accountable for our actions when we are under the influence of those drugs. We took the drugs to begin with. It was a decision. It was a karmic act.

The Sermon on the Mount is a treasure trove of the law of karma. Jesus states the mathematical precision of the law of karma: "With what judgment ye judge, ye shall be judged. And with what measure ye mete, it shall be measured to you again."[17] Short your neighbor on his bag of flour, don't give him the whole pound, and you will be shorted yourself—perhaps in bigger ways and more serious ways at a time that is very inconvenient for you, when you need all that you can get.

"Therefore all things whatsoever ye would that men should do to you, do ye even so to them. For this is the law and the prophets."[18] Jesus is saying that the Golden Rule, "Do unto others as ye would have them do unto you," is the law of karma taught by the prophets.

Jesus affirmed this law of karma taught in the Old Testament. Yet the Christian Church—from the Church Fathers all the way to the present leadership—has not acknowledged the record of Jesus' teaching on this subject. Rather, the prelates have vehemently denied it!*

## Breaking the Chain of Rebirth

The ascension is your soul's permanent reunion with God. When you attain that goal, you will have broken the chain of rebirth. I want to tell you that accomplishing this is hard work. But who among us has ever shirked from hard work? Hard work makes us what we are. If we're going to accomplish our victory in this life, we're going to have to roll up our sleeves, put our shoulders to the wheel and really get on with the balancing of negative karma through service to life and through invoking the violet flame (the sacred fire that transmutes the cause, effect, record, and memory of sin, or negative karma).

In every age men have asked the question: How do I break the chain of rebirth? The saints and sages of the Eastern religions have answered that question in many different ways. The Jains believe that you can destroy karma through purification, penance and austerity. Hindu theologians teach that you achieve liberation from the round of rebirth through the realization that the individual soul is one with the Absolute, or Ultimate Reality, called Brahman.

Hindu texts advocate the practice of different yogas as ways to attain union with Brahman. They teach the surrender to God, that this is the dissolution of bad karma and the creation of good

*For a complete explanation of Jesus' teaching on reincarnation and its suppression by the Church, see Elizabeth Clare Prophet with Erin Lynn Prophet, *Reincarnation: The Missing Link in Christianity*.

karma, and that it can free the individual from the bondage of karma and rebirth.

Surrender to God is a marvelous process. It is not a surrendering of free will but a commitment to use free will to affirm the will of God and to live it. It is a partnership with God. When we surrender to him, he doesn't take over our mind and soul so that we walk around like a wimp. When we surrender to God, we have access to him and we are working together for our own betterment and the betterment of our communities.

Gautama Buddha taught that in order to be liberated from the cycle of rebirth, called *samsara,* you must extinguish craving, or desire. He said inordinate desire is what causes *all* suffering and negative karma and results in rebirth.

The simple explanation is that when you desire something you do not have, you are acknowledging that you are incomplete, that you are wanting in something. If you affirm the wholeness of God where you are and affirm your joy in that wholeness, pretty soon you lose your desire for things outside of you and you are at peace in the completeness of the God within.

That's not to say we shouldn't have the normal things we need in life. That's not to say we shouldn't have happy homes and families and good relationships and whatever we need to carry on our mission. The problem is when there is a craving or desire for something that is inordinate and that is nonessential to our victory.

Take an example: You want something that somebody else has so bad that you start coveting it. You start getting upset that somebody has something that you don't. You start getting upset with God that he didn't give you what that other person has. You can get so upset about it that you devise a masterful plot of deceit to steal it from that person. Or, in the extreme, you can get so blinded by your lust, under the influence of alcohol or drugs, that you may even commit murder to gain your ends. Surely this is inordinate desire, which if undetected will cause you to lose your soul and, as Paul said, become "a castaway."[19] Why do you need all those things when God is inside of you, when the riches and the abundance of God are with you?

When you have inordinate desires that cause you to break the commandments of God in order to fulfill them, that cause you to violate the rights of others and the peace of others, you know that you are making karma. So you have to watch your thoughts and feelings and bring your life into alignment with the circumstances of your karma.

You need to accept your lot—your karmic lot! Whether it's to be poor or rich, what does it matter? We don't take our poverty *or* our riches with us into the kingdom of heaven in any case. What's important is that whatever our karmic circumstance, we express love to all in our circle of life, that we share with others when we have, and we depend on God when we have not. To experience the joy and the beauty of life, then, we must not have inordinate desires about anything, since inordinate desires inevitably cause us to sin.

## The Proof of Reincarnation

The doctrine of reincarnation cannot be separated from the doctrine of karma. They are twin doctrines. The fact that we make karma and must balance it, and that we continue to do so (until we learn the laws of God and stop making negative karma), means that we need the mercy of God, which he provides every living soul—yes, the mercy and the opportunity for reincarnation.

What would any of us do today if God had not given us life so that we could sow and reap his glory, his works, serve to set life free and balance our past karma? Once you realize the continuity of life, that the soul was not created when the present physical body was conceived, once you recognize that continuum and your own inner memory of an infinite past and an infinite future, you realize that in the scheme of things, it is impossible to become the fullness of who you are in one lifetime or to fulfill your mission, your reason for being.

When you realize that talents, hard work, achievement, good works, love and so forth are cumulative, just as evil is cumulative, you realize that everything you are today you have been building for centuries upon centuries and thousands of years. You have reached a pinnacle of opportunity, when civilization is at a height, when there is communication, when you can do the works of God and when we have the tremendous dispensations from God, such as the violet flame, the decrees, the intercession of the archangels and the ascended masters.

The absolute necessity for this cumulative experience is the reason why God set up the system of reincarnation in the first place! It was ingenious, expedient and powerfully practical. A single lifetime, whether lived to age 9 or 90 or 900, is just not enough time for the soul to mature to the levels required for her to achieve the crowning victory of individual Christhood.

Where is the ultimate proof of reincarnation besides in the Holy Spirit in your heart? It's in the living bible written in the sand, in the ethers, in the sea, in the marrow of your bones and in your inward parts. This record is called *akasha.** Akasha reveals in the aura of the individual and of geographical locations past life upon past life upon past life as well as group karma.

## The Past Lives of Public Figures

With this background, I will now take up the lives of some key people. I will go back into nine or more of their past lives. For some of these individuals I will give you their name in his most recent life at the beginning, and for some I will wait to the end

**Akasha* [Sanskrit, from the root *kās* "to be visible, appear," "to shine brightly," "to see clearly"] is an etheric substance and dimension, the subtlest, ethereal essence, which fills the whole of space. *Akasha* refers to the etheric energy vibrating at a certain frequency so as to absorb, or record, all of the impressions of life.

and allow you to guess who the individual is.

The information that I will present in the following chapters is a reading from the akashic records. It was taken under the direction of the ascended master El Morya, who selected the nine individuals for this study. This information was not obtained through hypnosis or psychic work but was released to me while I was in a fully conscious state.

I will begin with Henry Ford.

Henry Ford (1863–1947)

# CHAPTER 2

# Nine Lives of Henry Ford

*Genius is experience. Some seem to think that it is a gift or talent, but it is the fruit of long experience in many lives. Some are older souls than others, and so they know more.*

Henry Ford

Henry Ford lived on Atlantis. So did most Americans, if you believe the evidence of past-life regressions. Thousands of people, even those who have never heard of the lost continent, have reported having had lives there.

They flash on images of an ancient, technically advanced civilization where they, dressed in strange clothes, enjoyed a time of peace, advanced learning and high technology that has not been seen on earth since. In his readings, Edgar Cayce[1] frequently told people they had lived on Atlantis, tying their current problems to actions they had committed twelve thousand years ago and more.

Much of the speculation about Atlantis comes from references by Plato, the 4th century BC Greek philosopher. In Plato's *Timaeus,* which purports to be a conversation among Socrates and his friends, Critias tells a story he heard from his grandfather, who heard it from Solon, a famous Athenian lawgiver of the 6th century BC.

According to the story, an Egyptian priest told Solon about an island "larger than Libya and Asia combined" that had existed 9,000 years before in the Atlantic Ocean. But Atlantis had suffered a strange fate. The priest told him that Atlantis had been destroyed by fire, earthquakes and violent floods. "The island of Atlantis was... swallowed up by the sea and vanished," the priest said.[2]

Thousands of books have been written about Atlantis by people who say it explains everything from widespread flood legends to the similarity of plants and animals on both sides of the Atlantic.

Most scholars dismiss the story of Atlantis as the first work of science fiction, saying it is impossible for such a cataclysm to have taken place in relatively recent geological history. However, Jesus has revealed to me that Atlantis did, in fact, exist—and that what happened there holds the key to the unraveling karma of today's world. Many of those incarnating in America today have been waiting for thousands of years to return and right the wrongs they committed on Atlantis.

Why did they have to wait so long? Karma that is made with and between large groups of individuals in a technically advanced society cannot be balanced without the return to a civilization of corresponding level.

For example, if you were in an influential position in government or business or education on Atlantis and your decisions affected millions of people, you could not possibly reap the fruits of those actions until all of those people return to earth. If the civilization is destroyed, the soul must wait until an advanced civilization returns before he or she can balance that karma. You may have something good coming to you if you helped those millions of people, or you may have something to make up for if your decisions hurt them.

It has been said, and it is true, that America is Atlantis come again. Atlantis was a teeming continent with great advances in science and technology. Many of our scientists have brought back the same inventions that they developed on Atlantis. Many of the songwriters from Broadway were writing those same songs long ago on Atlantis.

Most of us lived on Atlantis and we are here to make right the mistakes of the past and to have our victory. Unfortunately, Americans today do not see themselves in the context of an ancient past that is being revisited upon us today. Nor do they understand that we can reach tremendous heights and achieve a golden-age civilization if we get right with God and our relationship to him, if we recognize that the Father-Mother God is also the indwelling presence and the Real Self of each one, the true Atman.[3]

My readings from the lives of Henry Ford begin with the soul's most recent life; in it we see the fruits of conflicts whose seeds had been planted thousands of years before.

## A Tangled Web of Karma

Henry Ford didn't know much about history. He thought the American Revolution was fought in 1812. But he was a mechanical genius who designed the first car for a mass market and quickly became one of the richest men in America.

He was born near Dearborn, Michigan, in 1863. His father was a farmer. His mother, who ruled the household with stern discipline, died when he was 13. He missed her terribly, saying that without her, the home was "a watch without its mainspring."[4]

She had supported his work with machines and believed he was a mechanical genius.

Henry found farming boring and preferred tinkering with machines to growing crops. He repaired the farm equipment and taught himself to fix watches and clocks. He felt alienated from his family. He later said that his father opposed his work except where connected with farming. He didn't get much support from the rest of the household; his siblings made fun of him for his strange hobbies.

After several years of conflict, at age 17, Henry went to Detroit and worked in a machine shop. He later moved back home but continued his preparation to be an entrepreneur, studying accounting, typing and shorthand at a Detroit business college.

In 1884, he met Clara J. Bryant, the daughter of a prosperous farmer, at a harvest moon dance. Thirty seconds after they started talking, he realized that she was the right mate for him. Practical and serious-minded, she believed in his ideas and supported his work with engines.

They married three-and-a-half years later and in September 1891 moved to Detroit, where Henry got a job as a mechanical engineer at a substation of the Edison Illuminating Company. They had one son, named after Henry's best friend, Edsel Ruddiman. In 1896, after years of tinkering with engines, he built his first car—the Quadricycle.

He got a group of investors to finance the Detroit Automobile Company in 1899, with himself as "mechanical superintendent." However, the company was dissolved the next year after Henry neglected work on design of the automobile. Henry's cantankerous and unpredictable attitude towards business dealings was to continue throughout his life. In 1901, he founded the Henry Ford Company, backed by five investors. Four months later, they fired him; he was building a racecar instead of putting a car into production.

Henry and Clara in the Quadricycle, Ford's first car

## Ford Motor Company

In 1903, with yet another group of investors, Henry Ford started the Ford Motor Company and built the Model A. This time, the company was a success. His investors got their money back within a year. But Henry wasn't content to be successful. He wanted absolute control. After some maneuvering, he gained a majority interest in the company and was soon able to put his grand idea into practice, to build a "car for the great multitude."

The Model T went on sale in 1908 and made him both wealthy and famous. It was faster, lighter and stronger than any car in its price range. "It was to provide America, and the world, with a whole new way of life,"[5] wrote biographer Robert Lacey.

By 1919, Ford had driven out the minority stockholders and divided the stock between himself (55 percent), Edsel (42 percent) and Clara (3 percent). This gave him unprecedented control—and wealth. By 1926, the *New York Times* estimated the Ford fortune at $1.2 billion (1926 dollars!).

The 1910 Model T. The car was a revolution in the automotive world. By 1918, half of all cars in the U.S. were Model Ts.

Early on, he treated his workers well. In 1914, he announced an unheard-of wage increase—to $5 per day. That was double the normal wage for auto workers. It also made sense for the company since it engrained loyalty in the workers. However, the workers had to meet strict standards of morality and cleanliness in order to earn their extra $2.66 per day. They were investigated by the paternal Ford Sociological Department with its faintly Orwellian tactics.

Ford's unpretentious attitude and support of the common man made him immensely popular in Middle America. Despite his great wealth, he did not join the club of America's financial elite. He mistrusted big banks and big government and opposed America's entry into World War I. The conflict benefited only the "absentee owners and parasites" of Wall Street, he believed.

Things did not always go his way. In 1916, he sued the *Chicago Tribune* for libel when it wrote an editorial calling him "ignorant." He lost the suit when the *Tribune's* lawyer proved he *was* ignorant by asking him many general-knowledge questions he could not answer correctly.

Henry Ford, Thomas Edison and Harvey Firestone.
These three American inventors were also friends on Atlantis.

He defined "ballyhoo" as "a blackguard or something of that nature" and said he thought Benedict Arnold, the Revolutionary War traitor, was "a writer." The moral of the story is: don't sue for libel if the story is true. The jury found that he *had* been libeled but awarded him only six cents in damages.[6]

The humiliation of the trial took some of the zip out of life for Ford; he became more introverted and focused on his company. He still found time for annual camping trips with his friends Thomas Edison and Harvey Firestone.

Around 1917, Ford had begun an affair with Evangeline Cote, a short, vivacious secretary at the Ford plant whom he soon promoted to his personal assistant. He directed her to marry his test-driver and installed them in a house near his estate so he could visit regularly. In 1923, she had a son, John, who was widely believed to be Ford's. Nevertheless, Clara still retained a strong place in his affections. "If I were to die and come back to another life," he said, "I would still want the same wife."[7] After some resistance, Clara accepted the arrangement.

## A Dual Nature

As many people have, Ford had a Jekyll and Hyde personality. On the one hand he was sunny and mild, on the other, he had, as one biographer described it, "hidden inclinations toward paranoia and ruthlessness."[8]

Oliver Barthel, who worked with Ford closely, said, "Mr. Ford seemed to have a dual nature. One side of his nature I liked very much and I felt that I wanted to be a friend of his. The other side of his nature I just couldn't stand. It bothered me greatly."[9]

His mean streak came to the fore in the early 1920s. He became a fanatic for absolute control. He fired his best men, some of whom went to work for his competitor, General Motors. One who was let go said: "If only Mr. Ford was properly assembled! He has in him the makings of a great man but the parts are laying about him in disorder."[10]

He was anti-Semitic and anti-Catholic. He reprinted and distributed anti-Semitic pamphlets, including the *Protocols of the Learned Elders of Zion,* a forgery that had been created by the Tsarist police to discredit Jews. Refusing to admit that he was hurting the Jews, he claimed that he was trying to change them. He thought that "good" Jews would appreciate what he was doing. However, he ultimately had to retract some of his statements and retreat from his stance. He publicly apologized for distributing the *Protocols* and said he had not known it was a forgery.

During the Depression of the 1930s, he was criticized for not giving more to charity. He vested more and more power in a former Navy boxer named Harry Bennett, who had started out in the company's art department but was soon transferred to security. Soon, Bennett was running what amounted to a private police force, the Ford Service Department. When hunger demonstrators marched outside the Ford River Rouge plant in March 1932, members of the Dearborn Police Department, under orders from Bennett, fired machine guns into the crowd, killing four men and wounding twenty.

A network of company spies reported on the workers for "crimes" ranging from wasting time to calling Ford names to attempting to unionize. In May 1937, four activists distributing union pamphlets were severely beaten by Bennett's thugs.

Although closed-minded in some ways, Ford was remarkably open in others. His interest in avant-garde ideas included a belief in reincarnation, including his well-known claim to have been a genius in a former life. Ford liked to give his explanation for why chickens scattered when a car approached: they had learned a lesson by having been "hit in the ass in a previous life."[11] Ford also believed he had died on a Civil War battlefield. He thought this experience had left such a deep imprint that it led him to oppose America's entry into World War I. "Every experience is worth having," he said. "Work is futile if we cannot utilise the experience we collect in one life in the next."[12]

Ford was attracted to both vegetarianism and alternative medicine, giving his chiropractor prominence over his medical doctors. He avoided red meat, chicken and sugar, promoted soybeans as the food of the future, and forbade the use of both alcohol and tobacco at his plant. When he and George Washington Carver met, after a brief discussion about diet, they went outside together, picked weeds, and proceeded to lunch on weed sandwiches, Carver's daily fare.

## Father and Son

Although Ford and Edsel were close while Edsel was growing up, Ford's cruel treatment of Edsel as he began to play a larger

Edsel Ford

role in the company is legendary. Edsel was a compliant son, and Henry despised this as weakness. To "toughen" him up, he countermanded his orders. Lacey gives one example of this:

> When Edsel commissioned a line of new coke ovens at the Rouge, his father outwardly appeared to go along with the decision, while confiding in the same breath to Harry Bennett, "As soon as Edsel gets those ovens built, I'm going to tear them down."
>
> The ovens were destroyed within days of their completion. Henry Ford could, obviously, have discussed the subject with his son in the first place, arguing it out face to face, or he could simply have countermanded Edsel's order there and then. But saying nothing and waiting to destroy the project until it reached fruition increased the pain—and hence the "therapy"—for Edsel.[13]

Although Edsel was made president of the company in 1918 at the age of 25, his father's fanaticism for absolute control was such that he could not relinquish control of the company. He refused to take advice, even when his decisions were having a negative impact on business. In the early 1920s, he ignored Edsel's suggestion that the Model T, which was outdated and becoming an object of ridicule, be redesigned. Ford waited to stop producing the car until 1927, when plunging sales forced him to take notice.

Meanwhile, he grew closer to Bennett and further apart from his son. Bennett had developed ties with gangsters and even gave them Ford contracts. Members of the Ford security force enjoyed the special perk of being allowed to siphon off spare parts. By 1943, the theft was valued at $1 million per year. The situation deteriorated as Ford grew older, suffering a mild stroke in 1938 and another in 1941.

All of this took its toll on Edsel. He suffered from a weak stomach and his father always blamed his ailments on drinking and rich living. Edsel's last battle was over the fate of the company purchaser, who had been attempting to stem the corruption instigated by Bennett. Despite Edsel's protests, Ford directed he be fired. In May 1943, Edsel took to his bed and, after several weeks, died. The diagnosis was a combination of undulant fever, ulcers, and stomach cancer, but those closest to him said he had died of a broken heart. He was 49.

Henry finally relinquished control of the company in 1945 after Edsel's widow threatened to sell her late husband's portion of the stock and thus take part of the company out of the Ford family ownership. Edsel's oldest son, Henry Ford II, took over the company. The elder Ford died in 1947 at the age of 83.

## The Past Is Prologue

As with most souls, Henry Ford's problems can be traced back thousands of years. The first of his lives that were revealed to me took place about 32,000 years ago.

---

**LIFE NUMBER 1:** Date: c. 30,000 BC
Sex: Male

A nomadic tribesman. He was captured by other tribesmen and forced to perform manual labor for the remainder of his "nasty, brutish and short" life. He spent most of his time lifting stones, carrying meat and cleaning skins. When he became too old to be useful, he was turned out of the camp at night and was eaten by wild beasts.

Note the beginning of the formation in his being of the need to be in control. "I have to be in control. I don't want anyone else to be in control of me, because look how that turned out."

---

**LIFE NUMBER 2:** Place: Atlantis
Date: c. 20,000 BC
Sex: Male

A farmer in the early days of civilization on Atlantis. Life was hard. There weren't many machines and he had to work very hard to earn a living. He had thirteen children and was generally a good father to them.

Atlantis, like other civilizations, had its alcoholic beverages. When he was drunk, he beat his children. Here is the inception of the recognition, "When I am drunk, I do things that I do not want to do." Thus, in his most recent life, he became strictly opposed to alcohol, not only for himself but also for his employees and his family.

His wife at that time was the same soul who later incarnated as Evangeline. One night, he beat her and pushed her down the steps. Pregnant at the time, she never recovered from the injuries and soon died.

Soon after, his farm was destroyed in a tornado. He and his family starved to death. This is an example of how harsh the lessons of life can be when divine intercession is not present. This experience left a deep impression on his soul.

---

**LIFE NUMBER 3:** Place: Atlantis
Date: c. 15,000 BC
Sex: Male

While the Atlantean civilization was still on the rise, the soul of Ford was born to a wealthy family in the capital city. His father, the same soul who later incarnated as Edsel, was then the Minister of Culture. But Ford was not interested in culture. He was interested in engineering and technology. The technology of the day was similar to that of 1920s America.

Henry, in partnership with the man who later embodied as Thomas Edison, developed the *naim*, a device similar to the television but capable of two-way communication.[14] He also developed a tornado warning system, harking back to his earlier misfortune delivered via tornado.

Freedom of the press was not part of Atlantean culture. Henry's father saw the usefulness of the *naim* as an instrument of culture, particularly of pro-government propaganda. Therefore, he introduced legislation (a prerogative of cabinet members in the Atlantean government) to nationalize the *naim* and allow no one but the government to manufacture or sell the device. The government was also the only one who was allowed to produce programming for the *naim* or to own the equipment to do so. Of course, this had the effect of stifling the free flow of information and development of culture on Atlantis.

Henry was devastated that his invention had been taken away from him. He thought it should be available to the common man to be put to its best use. He never produced another significant invention in that life. Crushed, he became estranged from his father (Edsel). This conflict was at the root of Henry's later desire to maintain control of the Ford company at all costs and, above all, not to turn it over to Edsel.

In his life as Henry Ford, his challenge was to finally forgive Edsel for his actions taken on Atlantis as his father. Henry needed to let go and surrender his possessiveness concerning the Model T and the Ford plant. But for all his genius, he was unable to pass this test.

As a result, Edsel was unable to fully pass his test, which was to work in harmony with his father and use his own talents to advance the company. He progressed in one sense by attempting to work with his father but failed in another by failing to stand up to him and choosing the escape of alcohol, which exacerbated his constitutional weakness of the stomach.

---

**LIFE NUMBER 4:** Place: Atlantis
Date: c. 13,000 BC
Sex: Female

Again he returns to the Atlantean stage as an inventor, this time a woman. She was short, with quick, dark eyes, a compact, capable body and incredible energy. She lived during a period of great technological development in which science had progressed much further than even in twentieth-century America.

She (Ford) was responsible for an innovation that allowed the flying car, called a *vailx*, to fly long distances over water. Previously, these *vailxs* had been able to fly, but only over land. They could not cross bodies of water but had to hug the coasts. This innovation opened up most of the world to Atlantean exploration and colonization.

She enjoyed a happy family life with her husband, a musician who was the soul later embodied as Evangeline. They had three children. Ford's twentieth-century wife, Clara, was embodied as a fellow scientist who helped with this invention. She worked hard and enjoyed fame and happiness. However, she never accumulated wealth because the patents for her inventions belonged to the government.

Notice how in two lifetimes, the soul of Ford invented something that benefited the public but failed to realize any personal benefit from it. Since what Ford created on Atlantis reduced drudgery and benefited all people, the public owed him something. Since the government took the patents on Atlantis, the government itself incurred a karma with Henry Ford.

So when he returned, he reaped the good karma of becoming a billionaire almost overnight. That was the income he deserved from many Atlantean inventions as well as for his development of the automobile. No one interfered with him having his just reward. This is the reason why I believe the free-enterprise system is important—it allows the law of karma to freely work.

This Atlantean life was also the source of his later interests in natural foods, chiropractic, and what we would call alternative health methods. Such approaches were the norm on Atlantis at this time, given equal partnership with medical science.

---

**LIFE NUMBER 5:** Place: Judah
Date: c. 895 BC
Sex: Male

He was a successful shepherd and devoted religious man during a dark period for the nation. Nine years after Solomon's death, about 924 BC, the ten northern tribes had revolted against Rehoboam, Solomon's son. They set up their own kingdom, Israel, with Samaria as its capital, leaving only two tribes under the control of the king at Jerusalem. The southern kingdom was called Judah.

Israel became prosperous and overshadowed, perhaps controlled, the smaller Judah. Both Egypt and Damascus threatened the weakened Judah. Egypt invaded, and Rehoboam paid a ransom from the temple treasury rather than fight. About 843 BC, Ahaziah, the king of Judah, was assassinated while visiting his relatives (by marriage) in Israel. Athaliah, his mother, seized the throne of Judah and executed all other possible heirs.

Athaliah, a daughter of the notorious Israelite queen Jezebel, promoted the worship of Baal, but there remained worshippers of Yahweh who dreamed of a restoration. Jehosheba, a sister of the murdered king, had saved his baby son Joash, and secretly raised him in the temple. Her husband, Jehoiada, a temple priest, organized a coup when Joash was seven years old. The palace guards executed Athaliah, and Joash restored the worship of Yahweh. According to II Chronicles, Joash "did that which was right in the sight of the LORD."[15]

The soul of Henry had been appalled by the direction the country was taking under Athaliah. He tried to be an example to others by being faithful to the letter of the law. He made positive karma in this area.

He made negative karma by being tyrannical to his family and servants. He refused to allow his oldest son to become a musician, forcing him to stay and tend the farm. Once, a boy lost some of his sheep and he beat the boy so badly that the boy developed a permanent limp.

In this life, Clara was again his wife. When you see souls returning lifetime after lifetime as partners, such as Henry and Clara, you begin to suspect that there is an inner bond between them much stronger than karma. This is often seen in the relationship of twin flames.

Each of us has a twin flame, someone whose soul was created at the same time we were and shares our soul blueprint. That one is truly our "other half," and often we find that one returning lifetime after lifetime to be with us. Paying off our karma of other relationships liberates us so that we can be with our twin flame.

In this life, the soul of Evangeline was incarnated as Ford's favorite daughter. He was good to her and balanced some of the karma he had made by killing her in lifetime number two.

The more you hear about these lifetimes, the more you will realize how important is the timing of the birth of every soul. Whom they will meet, marry, give birth to, who in turn their children will give birth to—it's a vast cosmic web.

It also tells us something about abortion. When we deny life through abortion, we are actually aborting the divine plan of a soul whose cue has been sounded to step forth on the stage of life to balance karma and help others. Abortion interferes with the karmic plan for millions of people who are supposed to be on earth at the same time so they can grow along with others of their generation.

---

**LIFE NUMBER 6:** Place: England
Date: 1763 to 1772
Sex: Male

Born to a Puritan family in England, he died of influenza at the age of 9. He loved his mother, the same soul who was to be his mother in his life as Henry Ford. His father was a businessman who was rarely at home. This life instilled in him the Puritan values he later championed.

The seven years between this lifetime and the next were spent in a part of the "heaven" world that is a realm of wish fulfillment (called *devachan*).[16] It is a place where people can create worlds for themselves to fulfill wishes, needs and desires they have had in their previous life. It allows them to experience the results of realizing their dreams without having to play them out while in physical embodiment.

This realm is meant to be a place of learning and soul growth. Some of these journeys can result in knowledge and attainment that one can bring to a future lifetime.

Ford's dream in this period was to take the best of Atlantis and design an ideal, moral society, one in which both bankers and government would have a limited role and the common man would have maximum freedom. We can see how he tried to bring these elements into play in twentieth-century America.

---

**LIFE NUMBER 7:** Place: Pennsylvania
Date: 1779
Sex: Male

His father was killed in the Revolutionary War. His mother raised him on a farm with six other brothers. All but one were the same souls who were his siblings as Ford. He was born with a twisted spine, which caused him to limp. This was his karma for beating the boy in his life as a Hebrew shepherd.

This shows us that it can take hundreds or even thousands of years between the time we commit a deed and the time we receive the karma for it. In Ford's case, it took about 2,500 years for that karma to come full circle. Sometimes God postpones our karma until we are mature enough to learn a lesson from it, to receive it positively and to see it as a way to pay our debts.

In this life, Ford's limp set him apart. In a foretaste of his Ford life, his brothers teased him because he was different. He allowed himself to be discouraged by their ridicule. At the age of 18, he left for Philadelphia. He got a job in the shipyards where he enjoyed drinking and carousing at night, staying single all his life.

He was mechanically talented and developed innovative ways to perform many tasks. Although destined to become a great shipbuilder, he didn't make use of his talents because he allowed himself to be discouraged by ridicule. His superiors and fellow workers laughed at his innovations and refused to try them.

Think about how many of us have been ridiculed by our playmates or our parents for having a unique or different idea. If we had paid attention to that ridicule, we would be nowhere. Only by having the courage of our convictions can we move on in life.

I always recommend that parents encourage their children to pursue the inclinations of their minds and hearts. When you understand that each child has a destiny and that the key to it may be locked in the child's heart, you will do everything you can to help him to unlock it, to unfold it from within. You also have a destiny locked inside yourself, which is why you should always have one ear listening to your soul, who, through her intuitive faculties, knows a lot more about you than you do at the conscious level.

So the soul of Ford allowed himself to be discouraged and failed to fulfill his destiny to become a great and innovative shipbuilder. One thing you should never do is allow others to discourage you from being who you are.

After death, the soul of Henry Ford vowed not to give in to discouragement in his next life. But first he had to pay off other karma.

---

| **LIFE NUMBER 8:** | Place: | Ireland |
|---|---|---|
| | Date: | 1824 to 1862 |
| | Sex: | Male |

You guessed it: a potato farmer. He was again married to Clara. They had eleven children, whom they brought up in a loving way. The family was poor but extraordinarily happy.

These were the same children he had beaten on Atlantis. He paid off his karma with them and earned his place in America, where he was to finally have the opportunity to return some of his innovations from Atlantis to the reincarnated Atlanteans in America.

## Another Opportunity—Another Life

So what has become of Henry Ford today?

We see that in his final life, he balanced old wrongs, enjoyed the fruits of his past life and created new wrongs he will have to reincarnate to make right. He will have to make amends to the family he tyrannized and to the workers he treated brutally.

Ford has not yet reincarnated.* He is studying in the universities of the spirit that are found in the heaven-world. And no doubt he is working on finally coming to grips with that two-sided self of his. He is trying to overcome his tendency to be ruthless and controlling with the truly loving soul qualities he has already developed.

And when he sets out to write the next page of his book of life, he plans to make better use of the opportunity.

*as of October 1992, when this lecture was delivered

CHAPTER 3

# Nine Lives and Another Chance

Let us take up the story of another soul, traced through nine past lives, so that we can better understand how karma outplays through our own lives. The reading from akashic records I am about to present is a slice of the evolution of a soul. We can all learn from the story of these nine lives tied together by karmic actions.

I'm going to keep you in suspense for a while about just who the twentieth-century incarnation is so you can enjoy guessing. You can skip ahead and peek if you want. But you might enjoy the reading more if you wait.

---

**LIFE NUMBER 1:** Place: Atlantis
Date: c. 18,000 BC
Sex: Male

This soul was born on Atlantis into a ruling family. He became a general and a benevolent dictator of a province. He was generally well-liked by the people until he imposed a new tax on a prosperous seaport. The tax was part of a new drive to raise money to build an elaborate new seat of government in the capital.

When he demanded ten percent of all revenues brought in by trade through the port, the town fathers refused. Next he sent in troops to arrest the fathers, but the people resisted. They were not accustomed to battles or fighting and they were badly beaten. To teach the rest of the province a lesson, the general ordered that everyone in the town be killed.

In this life, he was plagued by a deep sense of insecurity caused when his mother left his father, a well-known statesman. He was raised by a nurse who died. Although he tried to be a good ruler, he had difficulty trusting anyone. The incident with the seaport caused him to feel insecure and that he was losing control.

His mother had become a wealthy woman upon the death of the man she left his father for (a merchant). She lived in the town that he destroyed and was one of the leading opponents of the tax. This angered him. He saw it as a personal betrayal that she would oppose him publicly. When it came time to kill the citizens, not even she was spared.

---

**LIFE NUMBER 2:** Place: Atlantis
Date: c. 18,000 BC
Sex: Female

The soul was reborn as a girl into a respected Atlantean family with a rigid father and a liberal mother. Her father rejected his daughter after she was caught in bed with one of the servants. Psychologically, this act represented her attempt to get approval from the common people whom she had wronged in life number one. At the same time, she was emulating the mother who had abandoned her—in a previous life.

This soul had the opportunity in this life to make peace with her father and use her good fortune to become a humanitarian, serve the people and improve conditions for the poor. Instead, she chose to become a prostitute. She was forever seeking approval from father figures as a means of atoning for the wrongs of her past life. Eventually she became a wealthy madam who owned a chain of brothels. She enjoyed having power over other women (as their employer) and over men by knowing their secrets.

---

**LIFE NUMBER 3:** Place: Atlantis
Date: c. 18,000 BC
Sex: Male

This soul was given another opportunity to choose a higher path. He was born the third son of a poor, tightly-knit family in a fishing village. His mother and father loved each other and their nine children. The area was isolated, frequently overcast, rocky and subject to violent storms. On rare days when it was clear, it was a beautiful place.

The parents gave their children strict religious training according to the monotheistic religion of the time. They dedicated their third son to God. He became devoted and studied hard for the priesthood. He returned to his village and served for forty years as the village priest. Because of his efforts, the town knew a new piety and a closeness to God. Upon his death the townspeople considered him a saint. Many of these people were among those he had slaughtered in his previous lifetime, and he was able to repay some of his debt to them.

---

**LIFE NUMBER 4:** Place: Phoenicia
Date: 1289 to 1235 BC
Sex: Male

The soul was reborn into the slums of Phoenicia, the area occupied by present-day Lebanon. The Phoenician civilization flourished around 1250 BC. Their principal cities were Tyre and Sidon. This soul was given talents as an organizer and leader along with another chance to balance his karma by becoming a wise and benevolent leader.

Instead, he became a criminal who ruled over other criminals. Although he was kind to the poor, he took money from them and practiced brutal reprisals against anyone who opposed or betrayed him. He became a "Big Daddy" type who controlled prostitution and gambling. After he was stabbed to death by rival criminals, he realized that he had wasted his opportunities and resolved to do better in his next life.

---

**LIFE NUMBER 5:** Place: Italy
Date: Eleventh century AD
Sex: Male

He was the son of a servant in one of the great houses of a cardinal in Italy. He became a servant as well. He performed his duties well but was corrupted by the atmosphere of the times. He married and had children but abandoned them as he spent more time in his duties. He was given more important responsibilities and began taking bribes for allowing access to the cardinal. His life degenerated into drunkenness, greed and easy living. After several years of this, his wife took the children home to her family, leaving him alone to pursue his pleasures.

A pivotal incident in his life was when he was ordered to throw someone out of the palace and punish him for his forwardness. Angered at the man's lack of respect for his rank and position, he pursued him into the courtyard and beat him over the head with a stick. The man later died, although he had not intended to kill him.

As he grew older, he saw the emptiness of his life and tried to pay back those he had wronged. He became a hermit and died of old age.

---

**LIFE NUMBER 6:** Place: France
Date: 1298 to 1349
Sex: Male

He became a cardinal in the Catholic Church at Avignon, France. The Church was headquartered there from 1309 to 1377. The move took place after the Archbishop of Bordeaux, a province in France, was elected Pope Clement V.

The seven Avignon popes and their cardinals became notorious for their excess and love of luxury. Horrified critics throughout Europe compared the Church's exile in France to the captivity of the Jews in luxury-filled Babylon. The leaders of the Church increased the taxes and fees they collected in order to pay for their palatial residences as well as increased administrative costs. These included a tax ostensibly to support the Crusades, which had ended more than fifty years earlier, and huge fees for granting exemptions from church law.

Pope Clement VI built himself a palace on the Rhône River that the French diarist Froissart would later call "the finest and strongest building in the world."[1] Cardinals of the day lived more like princes than holy men. They had grand abodes along the banks of the Rhône with staffs of 150 servants. Although officially they were celibate priests, they generally had one or more mistresses and children whom the popes regularly legitimized. Other cardinals used their money to purchase handsome little boys.

Author Peter de Rosa writes about the life of a cardinal at Avignon: "Some cardinals had between four and five hundred of the richest livings [offices for which they received monies]. It meant they could afford the handsomest little boys, if they were so inclined, or the most beautiful ladies-in-waiting. Everyone in Avignon was well off: the musicians, the craftsmen, the bankers, goldsmiths, astrologers, pickpockets and the spectacular whores. Few complained that Bacchus and Venus were more honoured than Jesus Christ in Avignon."[2] Monks and friars who asked why the pontiff should live in luxury when Jesus had lived in poverty were tortured and burned by the Inquisition.

This soul began life with good intentions but was soon drawn into the round of luxurious living and endless taxation. He accepted and extorted bribes and became the essence of all that was corrupt in the Church—including buying and selling church offices. He failed to take the opportunity given him in this life—to help reform the Church.

He had several mistresses, one who loved him sincerely. She had been his mother on Atlantis and tried to make up for the wrongs she had caused him. He died when the bubonic plague swept the city of Avignon, killing over half the city. Filled with remorse for his wasted opportunity, he vowed to do better in his next life.

We can see two patterns thus far. First, that of missed opportunities leading to deathbed remorse. This can turn into a momentum that leads the soul one step forward and two steps backward. It becomes a rut that takes tremendous initiative to climb out of. The church doctrine of vicarious atonement—that Jesus paid for our sins—doesn't help much. It leads people to believe that everything will be alright provided they confess Jesus Christ as their Lord and Saviour. After you've done this a few lifetimes in a row, it becomes much harder to carve out a new destiny for yourself.

The second pattern we see is that of compulsive behavior stemming from feelings of abandonment. It led the soul into prostitution in one life and into vain attempts to seek approval in another life. This shows that the karma parents receive for mistreating their children can pile up from lifetime to lifetime as it ripples through their children's lives and the lives of those they touch.

As we will see in the next life, deathbed remorse can occasionally lead to genuine soul advancement.

---

**LIFE NUMBER 7:** Place: Sicily
Date: 1430 to 1490
Sex: Male

His name was Aloysius Rabata. He was born at Monte San Giuliano, in Sicily, and became a Carmelite monk at Trapani. He went on to become prior of the friary at Randazzo. In spite of his position of authority, he humbled himself with such tasks as repairing roads and begging for alms. Butler's *Lives of the Saints* says, "He lived on bread and water and was remarkable for his humility, his patience, and his zeal for souls." It recounts the story of how, when a poor man confessed to a theft that he could not pay back, friar Rabata went to the person he had robbed and asked forgiveness on the poor man's behalf.[3]

When he was 60, an unnamed assailant attacked him and beat him over the head. He refused to identify the man and he died soon after. The blow to the head paid off the karma from life number 5 when, as the cardinal's servant, he beat the man in Rome.

Aloysius Rabata was beatified by the Catholic Church in 1841. Today he is known as the Blessed Aloysius Rabata and his relics are in the collegiate church of Saint Mary at Randazzo.

It may seem ironic that a man who had been so corrupt in a previous life could turn around and become practically a saint in the next. It has to do with two things: first, the remorse he felt for having wasted his previous opportunity, and second, the character traits he was born with. This soul had earned the opportunity to devote himself to more spiritual pursuits. That doesn't mean he was predestined to live a religious life; it just means he had the tools to do it, and in this life he chose to use them.

---

**LIFE NUMBER 8:** Place: France
Date: Nineteenth century
Sex: Male

In this life he was meant to pay off more of his karma for the destruction of the town and its inhabitants on Atlantis. He was born into an extremely poor family where his father beat him, and his mother left home when he was small. She never returned. Without anything to anchor him, he took to the streets and became the victim of gang beatings.

Later he pulled himself together, became a well-to-do merchant, married and had five children. He devoted himself to his family. When he was in his early thirties, his wife and children were killed in a fire. For this he became angry at God and turned against Him. He decided at a very deep soul level to make his way without God.

Think about this. Nineteenth-century France is a predominantly Catholic nation, and he had been a good priest in his previous life. But Catholic doctrine did not teach him about karma and reincarnation. If it had been taught to him at his mother's knee and in his catechism, he would have looked at the death of his family as a natural outgrowth of that law—as both his karma and theirs. If the Church had given him that explanation, he would have had a better chance of dealing with his grief and pain and to have made a positive choice for his life. But he didn't. And it has affected his life ever since.

He became a smuggler and soon accumulated stockpiles of francs and gold coins. He was shot by a jealous competitor at age 39. After death he was still angry at God.

Death does not clear your life. It doesn't wipe it clean. It doesn't take all the chips off the gambling table. Everything is in place just as it was. The only difference between you now and you after the change called death is that you don't have a physical body. You still have your emotions, your memories, your mind. Anger, like other emotions, is carried through death and into the next life until the soul makes a conscious decision to change. Even then, the anger remains, and must somehow be purified or atoned for.

After death, as happens for everyone, he underwent a life review before seven beings of light filled with mercy and compassion. They are known as the Lords of Karma. During these reviews you can see every action you have committed during the past life as well as the effects of each act. What hasn't been brought out in any Near Death Experience (NDE) account I've seen is that you also see the karmic *reasons* based on your own past-life actions for why certain things happened to you. This is designed to help you understand the circumstances of your life and the lessons you were supposed to learn.

When this soul had his life review, he refused to learn from his past or even to look at his karmic record. So deep was his anger, he was not able to overcome it. He entered into his next life without the benefit of understanding his lessons at a soul level. What was that life?

If you haven't guessed by now, it's Alphonse Capone.

**LIFE NUMBER 9:** Place: United States of America
Date: 1899 to 1947
Sex: Male

This soul was given a mix of assets and liabilities when cast into a tenement house near Brooklyn's Navy Yard. On the one hand, he had intelligence, drive, charisma, organizational skill and concern for others that could have brought him to the top in any endeavor. On the other, he had anger, violence and an addictive personality that attracted him to a criminal life. And he had the egotism and flamboyance that became his downfall. He was a man who, in the words of biographer Laurence Bergreen, "confounded clear-cut definitions of good and evil."[4]

Al Capone was born January 17, 1899, in Brooklyn, New York. His parents, Gabriel and Teresina (Teresa) had emigrated to America five years earlier from the slums of Naples. Al had three older brothers, but he was to eclipse them all.

Although poor when they arrived in America, the family was neither starving nor penniless. Gabriel was able to make a decent living as a barber. In Al's older brother Ralph's words, the family "always had plenty to eat, good clothes to wear, and a good house to live in."[5]

At fourteen, Al's leadership qualities were already emerging. Angry because his mother's washtub had been stolen, presumably by Irish boys, he organized the Italian boys on his street. "We are the boys of Navy Street, and touch us if you dare!" they chanted as they marched through the street, luring the Irish out and giving them a beating.[6]

Al soon began running errands for the notorious gangster Johnny Torrio, whose Torrio Association was the prototype for the organized crime network that would unalterably change America's second largest city, Chicago. Capone said of him, "I looked on Johnny like my adviser and father and the party who made it possible for me to get my start."[7] Torrio was a new

Alphonse Gabriel Capone (1899–1947)

The young Al Capone with his mother, Teresa

kind of criminal, a precise and professional man who treated crime as a business. He emphasized cooperation over gang warfare, seeing it as the route to bigger profits for everyone.

Torrio kept a low profile, living in a modest apartment and remaining faithful to his wife. From him, Capone learned to keep his family life separate from his criminal activities and to present the appearance of respectability. Acquaintances remember Capone as quiet and well-mannered during his Brooklyn days. But he failed to copy his mentor's modest style after he became Chicago's biggest crime boss. Around this time, Al also began frequenting dance halls and prostitutes, and enjoyed pool playing and dancing.

At 18, Capone began work for a gangster named Frankie Yale as a bouncer and bartender at the Harvard Inn, a bar and dance hall on Coney Island. A fight he provoked by insulting a girl garnered him two scars on his left cheek and the nickname he hated, "Scarface." Soon after, Al killed his first man, a gambler named Tony Perotta, who owed Yale $1,500. As in other murders he would commit in his life, he was never charged or convicted.

But Al was also seeking stability and respectability. He met Mary Coughlin (Mae) in a club where Irish and Italians mingled. Tall, blond and slender, she worked as a salesclerk in a department store. She soon became pregnant and gave birth to Al's first and only child, Albert Francis, nicknamed "Sonny," on December 4, 1918. Three weeks later, he and Mae were married. Later on, Mae stayed at home and stayed out of her husband's social activities. She appeared content to maintain a respectable home life and, like Al's mother Teresa, ignore his other activities.

Although it seemed that his career as a gangster was about to take off, Al suddenly left the rackets and turned to legitimate business. He moved to Baltimore, where he worked as a bookkeeper for a construction firm. The business skills he gained here stood him in good stead as he later created the largest illegal business empire in the country.

Mae Capone with Sonny, Al Capone's only child

## On to the "City of the Big Shoulders"

In 1920, Al's father, Gabriele Capone, died of a heart attack, and soon after, Al went back to work for Johnny Torrio, who had moved to Chicago. Al quit his Baltimore job, borrowed $500 from his boss (which he later repaid) and went to Carl Sandberg's "stormy, husky, brawling" city. Torrio worked for "Big Jim" Colosimo, Chicago's premier brothel keeper. After Big Jim was killed, Torrio inherited his empire and expanded it to include thousands of brothels, speakeasies and gambling joints. The organization was earning about $3 million a year.

Al bought a home for his family and moved them all, brothers, mother, sister Mafalda, Mae and Sonny, to a peaceful middle-class neighborhood in Chicago. In 1923, Torrio took a trip to Italy, leaving Capone in charge of the organization. The new freedom brought out two traits that became part of Al's distinctive style: paternalism and flamboyance.

The Capone-Torrio organization had moved its base to Cicero, a suburb of Chicago where they could more easily control the government. In Cicero, Al first showed his ambitions of wanting to be more than just a racketeer. He wanted to pave the streets. He backed hand-picked candidates for the election to Cicero's Town Board.

In his insightful 1994 biography of Capone, Laurence Bergreen writes, "He did not simply want to corrupt or control the powers that be. He wanted to *be* the government, raking in money from the roulette wheel with one hand and spending it on public works with the other."[8]

The election took on what would become classic Chicago overtones. Capone's men intimidated and kidnapped voters and election workers, and a squad of police cars was sent to investigate. They encountered Al's older brother Frank on the street, and thirty or forty policemen converged on him. When he reached for his revolver, he was mowed down by dozens of bullets.

Johnny Torrio, the notorious Italian-American mobster, was Capone's mentor in his early years.

Frank's death gave Al another reason to want to be in control. It also made him the head of his family, superseding his older but less charismatic brother Ralph, and his oldest brother, Vincenzo, who had changed his name to Richard Hart and become a Nebraska Prohibition agent.

Al began to enjoy being in control of a million-dollar business. Bergreen believes that it was at this time that he began using cocaine, to which he would have had easy access. He bought an apartment building and turned it into a fortress for the exclusive use of himself and his closest henchmen. "It was here that he came with his pals and all their teenage mistresses to drink, to party, to make love until dawn and sleep to noon," writes Bergreen.[9]

On November 10, 1924, Capone and Torrio arranged for the first of the gangland executions that would continue to escalate in violence through the 1920s. The victim was Dion O'Banion, a rival bootlegger who refused to play by their rules and had turned Torrio in to the police for bootlegging.

O'Banion's death merely opened the door for more violence, and soon Al was fearing for his life, unable to go out without at least two bodyguards. Torrio was in danger, too. After rival gangsters made an attempt on his life, he decided to retire, leaving his empire to Al and the Capone family.

Before becoming the head of the underworld in Chicago, Capone had opposing Irish and Jewish gangs to fight off. Historian Richard Hammer wrote: "Capone's gang was tightly knit. And he had the drive and ambition that others lacked and the unscrupulous amorality to see him to victory. He was determined to be Chicago's master. To achieve his goal, Capone knew, he would have to smash his opposition unalterably, not with the Torrio technique of persuasion, treaties and compromise but in the manner he knew best, with violence."[10]

Understand now how this anger has been building over the centuries. And despite his role as the priest who was humble and served his people, he had never really resolved his anger against the mother figure who divorced his father, never resolved his feud with God for allowing his family to be destroyed in a fire.

These momentums do not just stay static. The entire accumulation of anger has been building from the moment his mother abandoned him on Atlantis to this time, when he determines he is going to become the master, he is going to play God, he is going to call the shots as to when people live or die. He will intimidate, he will persecute, he will cause people to fear and tremble and quake in their boots and in their beds. He will take that power from God and he will take it to himself.

## The Boss

Capone eliminated rival gangs one by one. Capone had little fear of official retribution, since gangland killings rarely resulted in convictions.

The twenty-five-year-old crime boss moved to a new headquarters at the Metropole Hotel, where he occupied nine rooms at $1,500 a day. He used it as his base until 1928. The move brought him more than luxury. It brought him publicity. He began seeking to appear like a legitimate businessman, giving interviews to journalists, posing for pictures, attending boxing matches and baseball games. Soon, everyone in Chicago knew who he was. Alva Johnston of the *New Yorker* called him "the greatest gang leader in history."[11]

Al tried to portray himself as someone who provided a public service, not a violent criminal but a benefactor. He was helped along by the hypocrisy surrounding Prohibition, in which everyone from the mayor to newspapermen and police regularly violated restrictions surrounding alcohol and frequented Al's speakeasies.

"Ninety percent of the people of Cook County drink and gamble," Al told reporters, "and my offense has been to furnish them with those amusements. Whatever else they may say, my booze has been good and my games have been on the square. Public service is my motto. I've always regarded it as a public benefaction if people were given decent liquor and square games."[12]

Capone didn't apologize for his violent way of life, but he liked to explain himself. "Well, maybe [a gangster] thinks that the law of self-defense, the way God looks at it, is a little broader than the lawbooks have it. Maybe it means killing a man who'd kill you if he saw you first. Maybe it means killing a man in defense of your business—the way you make the money to take care of your wife and child. I think it does. You can't blame me for thinking there's worse fellows in the world than me."[13]

As a businessman, Al acquired a good deal of finesse. During his summers in Lansing, Michigan, members of the Italian community remember him as a man of "class" and "grace," not "loud, flashy and coarse" as he was later portrayed in movies.[14] He was playful and loved children, buying them bicycles and handing out money. His newfound wealth gave him the chance to play Santa Claus—or God.

"From the huge roll of bills he always carried in his pocket," writes Hammer, "he would peel off $10 tips for news-boys and bootblacks, $20 for the hat-check girls or chambermaids, $100 for waiters [about $1,500 in today's money]. There was no end to his generosity."[15] Some saw him as a kind of Robin Hood, taking from the rich and giving to the poor.

"I'm not as black as I'm painted," he said. "I'm human. I've got a heart in me. I'll go as deep in my pocket as any man to help any guy that needs help. I can't stand to see anybody hungry or cold or helpless. Many a poor family in Chicago thinks I'm Santa Claus. If I've given a cent to the poor in this man's town, I'll bet I've given a million dollars."[16]

His generosity earned him almost reverential respect from the older generation. Anthony Russo (pseudonym), who knew him during his Lansing visits, described the gratitude of the community. "Anyone ever needed any help and who went to him and asked him for help got it. He was just that type of individual. Nobody ever gave him any special title, they never referred to him as 'Godfather,' they just called him Al. Except for the old Italians, that is. They respected his power, and when they were in his presence and he'd go over to shake their hand, they would kiss his hand because deep down they were afraid of him, see. To them he was always *Signore Capone.*"[17]

From governor to priest to cardinal, and now *Signore*. He had achieved the respect he had craved ever since the town on Atlantis had refused to give it to him. His desire to be thought well of and to be seen as a benefactor stems from that incident and ensuing massacre twelve thousand years before.

He spent hours helping people straighten out marital difficulties. He paid their medical bills. "I don't know what he gained by being kind to those kind of people because they couldn't do anything for him; he was doing it for them," commented Russo.[18] What he gained were loyal strongholds of Italian supporters.

Despite his Robin Hood persona, much of Capone's money

came from those that could ill afford to lose it. By the end of 1928, according to the attorney general's office in Illinois, ninety-one of Chicago's unions and trade associations were controlled by racketeers. "The cost to the public was enormous. When Capone moved in on the cleaning-and-dyeing industry, in order to raise the protection money, the merchants had to raise the price of cleaning a suit by 75 cents; when he moved in on the kosher butchers, the price of corned beef went up 30 cents a pound. By the end of the decade [the 1920s], the Mob's control was costing consumers in Chicago $136,000,000 a year, or $45 for every man, woman and child," writes Hammer.[19]

Of all the gangs in Chicago, Capone's had the biggest chunk of the action. His empire took in about $105 million in 1927, according to estimates of the U.S. attorney's office. Sixty million dollars was from alcohol, the rest from gambling, prostitution and other rackets.[20]

In 1928, Al moved his headquarters to even more luxurious surroundings, the Lexington Hotel, where he rented the entire fourth floor and most of the third floor. Capone had a six-room suite which cost $18,000 a year. There were other suites for his women. Capone had a private kitchen installed by the hotel and a private chef, who tasted all food and drink before it was served. Capone devised an elaborate secret escape route that went from the hotel through the adjoining office building. In all of these precautions, we see him trying to insulate himself from his own returning karma.

## A Spiral-Shaped Bacterium

In 1928, Capone was at his most powerful. He controlled the police, the mayor and much of the city and county government. But the seeds of his downfall were present. Despite his wealth and his efforts to maintain control over his life, a spiral-shaped bacterium was eating away at his nervous system—and determining his destiny. When his mistress was diagnosed with syphilis, he received a warning of what was to be his fate. But he refused to be tested, fearing doctors and needles.

Bergreen believes Capone may have contracted syphilis in 1915, when he was frequenting prostitutes in Brooklyn. The disease that would later kill him comes in three stages. Only the third is fatal, and it returns in only 20 percent of cases. But the latency period between the second and third stages can be as long as twenty years. Al may have thought he was cured after the flu-like symptoms of the second stage disappeared.

Signs of the disease began showing up in his public behavior. Although he kept a firm grip on his empire, he became prone to fits of anger, lost huge amounts of money gambling, and drifted farther from reality in his public statements.

In one interview, he embarked on a flight of fancy, claiming he had never killed anyone and never "directed anyone... to commit a crime." He called Cicero "the cleanest burg in the U.S.A.," saying it had only one gambling house and not a single "vice den."[21] Capone lost hundreds of thousands of dollars gambling at Florida's Hialeah Race Track. He destroyed golf clubs during games with his bodyguards. "He became ever more temperamental—by turns gloomy, ebullient, and violent—without apparent cause," writes Bergreen.[22]

Capone had made deals with or subdued most of the rival gangs in Chicago. But the Bugs Moran mob repeatedly attempted to assassinate him and succeeded in wounding one of his bodyguards, "Machine Gun" Jack McGurn. While Capone was in "retirement" in Florida, members of his gang carried out the most famous gangland massacre of the time.

On Valentine's Day, 1929, a stolen police car pulled up outside the garage that was used by the Moran gang. Four men rushed out, two in police uniforms. Five members of the Moran gang and two of their associates were in the garage. The men in police uniforms ordered Moran's men to line up against the wall. Thinking it was a routine police raid, they obeyed. The assassins then disarmed Moran's men and opened fire. Although no one was brought to trial for the crime, the public attributed it to Capone.

Mug shot of Capone in Florida, 1930

In May 1928, Capone got word that two of his own lieutenants, Scalise and Anselmi (gunmen who are suspected of having participated in the St. Valentine's Day Massacre), had changed their loyalties. To test them, he staged an argument with a trusted lieutenant, Frankie Rio. They soon approached Rio and invited him to join a plot to kill Capone. Capone soon invited Scalise and Anselmi to an elaborate dinner with a hundred of his "closest allies." After Scalise, Anselmi and their co-conspirator, Joseph "Hop Toad" Guinta, had eaten and drunk all they wanted, his aides surrounded them, tied them to their chairs, and Capone beat each of them nearly to death. A group of gunmen then finished them off.

This episode was uncharacteristic of Capone, who preferred to distance himself from violence. Whether this and other similar outbursts were induced by syphilis or whether they were simply part of his character, their root cause was his unresolved anger against God dating all the way back to Atlantis. He was accountable for those outbursts and murders, just as we are all accountable for the harm we do to any part of life, whether it is based on our childhood psychology, our difficult circumstances, past lives or an advancing disease.

By early 1930, times had changed for Capone. His flamboyant behavior along with the escalating violence had gained him the attention of the Federal government. And his public support eroded as the Depression deepened.

At the end of 1930, Capone, sensitive to the disfavor with which the public was beginning to view him, opened a soup kitchen for the Depression's hungry. The "army of ragged, starving men" who showed up three times a day were great PR for Capone. They told the press that Capone was doing more for the poor than the government was.

But what Capone gave to the poor with one hand, he took with the other. The same year he started the soup kitchen, Capone raised the wholesale price of beer in Chicago $5 a barrel, from $55 to $60. His cost remained the same, at $4 a barrel.

Unemployed men queue outside the soup kitchen opened in Chicago by Capone, February 1931.

Meanwhile, the government was catching up with him. In 1927, the Supreme Court had issued a ruling that was to have disastrous effects for Capone. Illegal earnings, such as those garnered from gambling and bootlegging, were now taxable. The IRS had set up a Special Intelligence Unit to investigate such cases, and it began closing in on Capone.

They indicted his brother Ralph for income tax evasion in 1929. Although Ralph offered to pay up, they refused his offers, preferring instead to continue their investigation. He would be a test case before they went after the big fish.

## A Slippery Ride to the Bottom

As the income-tax noose tightened, Capone failed to understand the gravity of the situation. Ralph went to trial and was found guilty on all counts. He faced up to twenty-two years in prison and $40,000 in fines.

The IRS refused Al's offer to pay up. Their case against him was growing and on June 5, 1931, a federal grand jury indicted him on twenty-two counts of income tax evasion. His back taxes amounted to $215,080.48. Capone tried to make a deal with the IRS and the U.S. attorney general. He pleaded guilty, thinking he had a deal, but the federal judge refused to honor the agreement. Capone changed his plea to not guilty, and the trial preparations went forward. It was the beginning of the end of his carefully built persona.

After his indictment, the public had even less sympathy for him. The jurors at his trial, largely rural, conservative men, over 45, could be counted on to feel indignant at Capone's lavish lifestyle. The testimony included information about Capone's spending habits, the twenty-three suits he had bought in Marshall Field, shirts by the dozen, and union suits (undershirts and shorts) made of Italian glove silk.

On Saturday, October 17, the jury returned a verdict of guilty on five of the twenty-two counts. Seven days later, the judge sentenced him to eleven years in prison plus $50,000 in fines and $30,000 in court costs.

Capone appealed the verdict while sitting in a luxuriously furnished cell in Cook County Jail, serving highballs to visitors and ruling his empire as usual. When the newspapers discovered that the prison warden was using a black, 16-cylinder Cadillac registered to Mae Capone, the government determined that he should serve his sentence far from his sphere of influence in Chicago.

He was sent to the federal penitentiary in Atlanta, Georgia. It was there that for the first time he was diagnosed with neurosyphilis, which was beginning to have more noticeable effects. Although he was a placid prisoner, his fellow inmates noticed alternate bouts of brooding or ranting.

The new U.S. attorney general's pet project was to create a maximum-security facility at Alcatraz Island in San Francisco Bay. Capone, as one of the government's most celebrated prisoners, was earmarked to be one of its first inmates. In the summer of 1934, he was transferred.

At Alcatraz, Capone hardly appeared the confident gangster of days gone by. He was "amiable, docile, and touchingly eager for the good opinion of all," Bergreen writes.[23] He started a band composed of Alcatraz inmates and later taught himself to play the banjo and the mandolin.

On February 5, 1938, he suffered a breakdown from which he never fully recovered. He went into convulsions and was confined to the prison hospital ward. He told the doctor he heard God and angels replying to his prayers and detailed good works he would embark upon on his release, including charity work and starting factories to employ the poor. Perhaps his deathbed remorse was kicking in again.

The federal penitentiary on Alcatraz Island, San Francisco. Al Capone was its most famous inmate, held there from 1934 to 1939.

In November 1939, he was released from federal prison due to his deteriorating mental and physical condition. He received penicillin for treatment but had already suffered extensive brain damage. He lacked mental and physical coordination and suffered periods of disorientation, unintelligible speech, tremors and epilepsy-like seizures. He died on January 25, 1947, in Miami, at age 48.

The tragedy of his life is that he was unable to overcome the deep-seated momentums stemming from his past lives. The need for power and control ultimately became his downfall. The vulnerability and quest for approval were equally responsible. His flamboyant lifestyle was part of his search for public acceptance. But it also attracted the government's attention and helped to bring about his demise.

But regardless of how he chose to spend his life, the disease that contributed to his downfall had entered his life as early as 1915. Being angry with God puts the soul in a position of vulnerability. The pockets of anger left over from previous lives made him vulnerable to the deadly third stage of syphilis. The anger is often sealed in the unconscious and it comes out in many different ways. It can attract disease and even aberrations in the personality, lifetime to lifetime.

That's why it's important for each of us to get right with God by resolving our personal psychology and being willing to dig until we get to the root of our problems with a good, qualified therapist. Only by daring to look at the deepest parts of ourselves can we discover and overcome the elements that make us work at cross purposes with ourselves.

## The Mercy of God

Before we leave the story of Al Capone, let us hear the mercy of God. Even he—murderer, pimp, bootlegger—gets another chance. It may not be the chance we would want for ourselves, but it is a chance.

Al Capone has reincarnated in the slums of Bangladesh. He has received the gift of life. Some of us would consider such a life to be worse than hell. We might not want such a life. But what is important about it is that he has received the gift of life and the chance to make good.

Isn't such a chance, any chance, better than the one-shot deal of Christianity? And doesn't the fact that God would give such a soul another chance give hope to us all?

CHAPTER 4

# The Diaries of a Narcissist

---

**LIFE NUMBER 1:** Place: Atlantis
Sex: Female

She was the Chief of the Ministry of Culture on Atlantis. She became upset when the high priest refused to endorse her art. He said it was not a proper representation of the Divine Source. She left the high priest's quarters in anger, vowing henceforth to never glorify God or God in man but only man in himself. This sets the sail for everything that has followed from this ancient time to the present day. Under her tenure, the culture of Atlantis was perverted.

---

**LIFE NUMBER 2:** Place: Atlantis
Sex: Female

She was a priestess on Atlantis, a "vestal virgin." She sought the priesthood specifically out of revenge for the slight against her in her previous life. Perhaps she was consciously aware of this motive, perhaps not. These momentums of anger and revenge do carry over from one life to the next, and you don't have to even remember the previous life to carry the vibration of revenge.

She became very close to the high priestess and then turned against her. She set up another temple where people came to worship themselves. She set up a new religion that was a perversion of what we know today as psychoanalysis. People tried to perfect themselves through themselves.

There are people today who espouse this same philosophy. Ma Anand Sheela, the right arm of the Indian guru Rajneesh, was once asked on a talk show, "Whom do you worship?" She said, "We worship ourselves."

---

**LIFE NUMBER 3:** Place: Ancient Egypt
Sex: Female

She was the daughter of a nobleman in ancient Egypt. She became High Priestess in the temple of Isis.

---

**LIFE NUMBER 4:** Place: Ancient Greece
Sex: Male

He was born in a farming community in ancient Greece. He was the only son of poor farmers. His test in life was to sublimate his own desires and support his parents. He abandoned his parents and went to Athens. He became a well-known sculptor. He had an affair with a slave woman. He forced her to kill the baby daughter who was born to them.

His art glorified the human rather than the divine. He never sent money to support his parents. They died impoverished. He never married because he did not want to share his success. But it did not last and he died forgotten.

---

**LIFE NUMBER 5:** Place: Corinth
Sex: Male

He was born in Corinth, a city in southern Greece, and became a wealthy slave owner. He married a woman who would incarnate as the subject's father in her final embodiment. He saw another woman who was also to be a key figure in her final embodiment. She was a courtesan to the ruler of the city. He risked his life to have sex with her. He was not caught. Then he arranged the death of both his wife and the ruler of the city. He took the courtesan as his wife.

---

**LIFE NUMBER 6:** Place: Spain
Date: 1600s
Sex: Male

He was born in Spain in the 1600s as an ugly boy, a hunchback. His father hated the sight of him. His mother loved him. His mother was the soul who later incarnated as his loving spouse. He fell in love with a beautiful girl, the courtesan from his past life. She married someone else. He engaged in perverted sex with prostitutes. He never married. He could not stand the sight of his own ugliness. He never engaged in anything useful. He died poor.

---

**LIFE NUMBER 7:** Place: Holland
Date: 1690 to 1765
Sex: Female

She was born into a wealthy family in Holland in 1690. She used her position to promote arts and culture. Two of her children would feature in her most recent life. She was a good mother to them. She was a positive force in the community in that she promoted beauty and the arts. She also squandered much energy on affairs with artists she supported, wasting her life-force.

When you waste your life-force and spend it extravagantly, you don't regroup that force in each new lifetime. You have less and less. And squandering the life-force has its cumulative effect, which manifests in all kinds of problems—mental weakness, physical weakness, ineffectiveness, inability to do what one needs to do.

Through her positive efforts, she earned the opportunity to be a talented artist and writer in her next life.

**LIFE NUMBER 8:** Place: Ukraine
Date: 1860 to 1884
Sex: Female

Marie Bashkirtseff was born November 11, 1860, in the Ukraine to a Russian family of wealth and nobility. Her mother left her father after two years of marriage, took the two children, Marie and her brother, and returned to her parents. In the household were Marie's grandmother and an aunt.

In 1870, she left Russia with her mother and brother and extended family. She was in command of the family. She spent her childhood years traveling between Baden-Baden, Paris, Nice, Rome and Naples. She was well-educated. She learned several languages including Greek, Latin and Italian.

Marie Bashkirtseff, 1878

"Her library contained 700 volumes, and she read them all, often at the dinner table, devouring 'moderns' like Daudet and Flaubert" while also reading the classic works of "Confucius, Michelet and Montesquieu," writes author Gwyneth Cravens.[1] She studied voice and the mandolin. At age 12, she began her journal in French. She was beautiful and had many suitors. She admired herself greatly. She wrote: "I looked all of a sudden so beautiful, after I had taken my bath this evening, that I spent fully twenty minutes admiring myself in the glass."[2]

At age 17, she began studying painting in Paris. She pledged in her diary: "At twenty-two I shall be either famous or dead.... I swear that I will become famous; I swear solemnly—by the Gospels, by the passion of Christ, by myself—that in four years I will be famous."[3]

She seriously devoted herself to art for the rest of her life "following a rigorous and highly disciplined regime of work."[4] The Paris Salon awarded her two *mentions honorables*. She began a painting of the Virgin Mary and Mary Magdalene weeping at Jesus' tomb, which she called *The Holy Women*, hoping it would be her masterpiece.

She had a passionate love of life. She wrote: "To think only *that we live but once,* and that this life is so short! When I think of this my senses forsake me and my mind becomes a prey to despair! *We live but once!* And I am losing this precious life, hidden in obscurity, seeing no one. *We live but once!* And my life is being ruined. *We live but once!* And I am made to waste my time miserably. And the days are passing, passing, never to return, and carrying a part of my life with them, as they pass."[5]

This is the lament of someone who has repeatedly squandered their life-force. It is also the lament of those who suspect that they might not be immortal because they have not sealed their covenant with God. And so when they know that life is passing, they know it is passing for good because that original vow stands, that vow to move against God.

She was ambitious. When one of her paintings was acknowledged, she said it was not enough. She wrote, "Yes, when my name is mentioned every voice must be hushed, every head turned in my direction, in order to satisfy me."[6]

Earlier she had written, "Am I culpable in desiring to be great? No, for I desire to employ my greatness in manifesting my gratitude to God, and in being happy. Is it forbidden to wish to be happy?"[7]

We understand that the use of the terms *Christ, God,* and so forth, may simply be the product of a religious upbringing, the product of the times in which someone lives. Simply because people recite these words does not mean that in their inner soul of souls, in their inner beings, they have in any way renounced their original determination to move against God. We have to judge people not by their words but by their vibrations, their fruits.

On October 31, 1884, she died in Paris of tuberculosis. She was 23. Her diary was published and became famous. William Gladstone, the British Prime Minister, called it "a book without parallel."[8]

---

**LIFE NUMBER 9:** Place: France
Date: 1903 to 1977
Sex: Female

Anaïs Nin, well-known author and diarist, was born on February 21, 1903, in Neuilly, France (a suburb of Paris). She received a strict Catholic upbringing. Her father was the Spanish composer-pianist Joaquin Nin. He spent his time womanizing and traveling the concert circuit. During his sporadic visits home, he argued with his wife and sometimes criticized and abused Anaïs and her brothers, Thorvald and Joaquin. In the second volume of her unexpurgated diaries, published in 1992 and titled *Incest: From "A Journal of Love,"* Nin revealed that she had had an incestuous relationship with her father.

Anaïs Nin (1903–1977)

Nin's father exposed her to books and music and whetted her appetite for the artistic life. Her parents frequently moved and traveled throughout Europe. When Nin was 11 years old, her father deserted the family for a very young woman. Joaquin was the same soul she had been married to and murdered so that she could marry the courtesan.

In 1914, she left Barcelona, Spain, for New York with her mother and two brothers. On the voyage, she began keeping a diary. It became her lifelong occupation. At first, she said, she wrote in order to persuade her absent father to return.

In 1919, she dropped out of high school. She was taken to Cuba by a wealthy aunt. There she met and married Hugh P. Guiler, a banker. She called him Hugo. They went to France. In 1929, they settled in an old house in Louveciennes, just outside of Paris. Their home became a gathering place for unknown writers and artists who would later become famous.

## Relationship with Henry Miller

Both Hugo and Anaïs believed in promoting literature about sexual liberation and living life to its fullest. In 1931, she met Henry and June Miller, an American couple in Paris. She wrote in her diary: "I'm singing! I'm singing! And not secretly but aloud. I've met Henry Miller. I saw a man I liked... a man who was likable, not overbearing but strong, a human man who was sensitively aware of everything. He's a man whom life makes drunk.... He is like me."[9]

Her relationship with Henry began with a casual lunch. After a few months of intellectual discussions, the relationship turned into a tumultuous love affair. Henry and Anaïs were never able to establish a life together, but remained tied to each other nonetheless. They shared a passion for writing. Henry's wife, June, who lived in New York, visited him in Paris periodically.

Henry Miller, 1940

Anaïs and June were passionately involved from December 1931 to January 1932 and for a few weeks in October 1932. It is unclear whether they had a physical, sexual relationship. Nevertheless, Anaïs was obsessed with June, as was Henry. June was a beautiful and sensuous woman who was adroit at living multiple lies. She almost never told the truth. She took other people's stories and made them her own. She was tawdry and egotistical. She was a mooch. She fought with Henry and criticized his work.

Anaïs later said, "It seemed to me that my love of June was really not *for* June; she was the woman *I* wanted to be. There was this attraction to a projected part of myself. It was really identification; I realized that we were not two people, but that she was really the woman I wanted to be. I felt that it was a narcissism."[10] June was the courtesan Anaïs had desired in two lifetimes.

Anaïs's relationship with June lasted only a few weeks. Henry divorced June and she moved back to the United States. Henry and Anaïs continued their affair through most of the 1930s and remained lifelong friends.

Nin and Miller saw themselves pioneering the sexual revolution. Both used fiction to explore the nature of eroticism. A 1990 movie called *Henry and June* tells the story of this strange triangle. According to Gunther Stuhlmann, editor of Nin's diaries, the movie is not accurate and is "just Hollywood."[11]

Despite her affairs, Anaïs stayed married to Hugo. Later he illustrated her books under the name Ian Hugo. She wrote: "Every word I wrote about Hugo [who appears as a character in one of her stories] reveals his youthfulness and the religious aspect of my love for him. I write about him as one writes about God, with traditional faith."[12]

In 1932 she wrote *D. H. Lawrence: An Unprofessional Study*. It was her first book. Lawrence is well known for his novels glorifying sexual fulfillment. He held that industrial culture dehumanizes and believed man should return to his roots in nature to find happiness. His writing is sexually explicit and his book *Lady Chatterley's Lover* was long banned.

In 1933, Anaïs was reunited with her father. The reunion was a disappointment as she realized that her father would never overcome his weaknesses.

After World War II began, Anaïs moved back to New York. In 1942 she set up her own printing press because of her difficulty in finding a publisher. She published novels and short stories. But it wasn't until 1966, when the first volume of her journals was published, that critics began to regard her as an important writer. She became a patron saint for many women in the sixties. She died of cancer in Los Angeles in 1977.

## The Religion of Psychoanalysis

If Nin had a religion, it was psychoanalysis. She began psychoanalysis in 1932 with Dr. Rene Allendy. He was the first of four psychoanalysts she worked with. According to author Nancy Scholar, throughout her life, Nin "maintained her adherence to the 'modern religion' of psychoanalysis, believing it to be the 'key to all other experiences,' the 'only way for us to achieve wholeness.'"[13]

Nin was accused of being narcissistic for keeping a detailed diary. She was also accused of living her life only so that she could have experiences to write about. She believed the diary was necessary for her growth. Defending herself, she said: "Those who misunderstood the *Diary* were the ones who were so obsessed with the idea that any introspection, any regard for individual growth, any concern with one's personal conflicts was narcissistic.... The self has to merge with the collective interests or general humanity, but first of all it has to *exist* in order to be able to make a choice and to make a contribution."[14]

She also said: "There is a realm in which you are all-powerful, in which you are the captain of your soul. And ultimately this cell that you work at connects with millions of other cells. You project your inner reality into the external. But first you have to make your psychic core a reality."[15] She believed that she wrote on behalf of many women and that her diary would be a mirror for others to look into their own souls.

Later in life, she said that she had resolved her problems through psychoanalysis and had attained a sense of reality, maturity, peace and joy. She said that she was liberated from her ego.

## Nin and Bashkirtseff

Anaïs Nin read Bashkirtseff's diaries as a girl and was astonished by some of the similarities with her own diary. She wrote, "There are things she says that are reflected word for word here in my own diary. It's enough to make me think I am mad and that I copied them—or else that Marie's soul has been reincarnated in me!"[16]

The women have much in common, but Nin appears to have lived on a deeper level. Author Nancy Scholar writes, "The similarities between the two are remarkable, including an early craving for fame and admiration, along with a penchant for mirror-gazing. But Marie's blatant self-satisfaction with her reflection is unthinkable to the young Anaïs, more ambivalent about her self-image and possibly more aware of her audience at this age."[17]

Bashkirtseff falls more into the definition of narcissism than does Nin. But the quality that they both share is the quest for passionate living without God. Even though Bashkirtseff pays lip service to God, it is clear that her God is her self with a lowercase "s" instead of her Real Self, who is God.

This is not a theme exclusive to Nin. As Oliver Evans wrote in his book about Nin: "Miss Nin's favorite theme—the quest for self, the search for identity—has come to dominate much if not most of the serious fiction which has been written in the last three decades; it is a contemporary obsession."[18]

## The Folly of Self-Worship

Anaïs Nin is a profile of a certain type of person. She taught people to worship themselves. The end of this type of self-worship is nihilism or self-annihilation. You become coiled up in yourself. When you get all coiled up, that is the end. There is nothing at the center of the coil.

El Morya selected Nin as a study for us so that we could know the folly of self-worship. This folly did not die with Anaïs Nin. It is a widespread disease in America—and the world—today.

Let's look again at this quote. She is defending her position on the very fine line where truth meets error, where absolute Truth meets absolute Error. She first says that people misunderstood the *Diary* and those who did were so "obsessed with the idea that any introspection, any regard for individual growth, any concern with one's personal conflicts was narcissistic."

Well, of course, it is not. We have to take hold of ourselves. We have to know who we are. A certain amount of analysis and studying our psychology is indispensable to the spiritual path. This we do with God, not without God. We do not do it with the human God that we have made of ourselves. We do it with the true divinity of God who has placed a portion of himself, the divine spark, in us. So this is a meaningless defense.

She says, "The self has to merge with collective interests or general humanity, but first of all it has to *exist* in order to be able to make a choice and to make a contribution."

Mark Prophet taught me that sometimes we first have to be selfish in order to be generous. And what he meant by this is that we have to give enough attention to ourselves so that we know ourselves as a whole person, so that we have the education, the talents, the ability, the inner drive and the balance of love and wisdom and power in our world that we can turn around and give ourselves to our families and to the larger good of humanity.

This is the homeward path to God. When we are learning in school, we are putting all of our attention on ourselves so that when we are fully grown and ready to take our place in society, we will be a balanced personality. The term here is "an integrated personality in God" whereby our personality reflects clearly in a balanced way some aspect of the personality of God.

To make that contribution, we have to concentrate on ourselves for a time. But even while we are doing that, while we are growing up, our parents teach us to help others, to be service-minded, to become Girl Scouts or Boy Scouts or to be in organizations where the welfare of people beyond our family is our concern.

That is the American way of life, and most of us have that in our background.

The next statement Anaïs Nin makes is, "There is a realm in which you are all-powerful, in which you are the captain of your soul." Judging from her point of origin and take-off in rebellion against God at the altar of Atlantis, her realm where you are the all-powerful is in the supreme moments when you feel your ego to be in absolute control of you and everyone else. This is what I intuit she is talking about as being "the captain of your soul."

The real captain of your soul, of course, is your mind one with your Holy Christ Self. But you are not only the captain of your soul; you are the Father-Mother of your soul, and you are also the student of your soul.

"Ultimately this cell that you work at connects with millions of other cells." This is true. It is true that we connect with one another, especially those on the same path, the same wavelength, the same karma.

"You project your inner reality into the external." Yes, you project the flame of God that is in you, the flame of life, the flame of reality into the external world and you make the world a better place.

Then she says, "But first you have to make your psychic core a reality." Yes, you have to be aware of your psyche, your soul, and the soul's needs must be met. And this is the resolution we must attain with our human parents, with our human surroundings, siblings, the things that happened to us in our early development. We don't react against people who have mistreated us, but we learn to love and to transmute, to forgive and to recognize our karma when we see it coming our way in the person of our closest relatives, even our parents.

She is quoting timeless truths. And this is, shall we say, the height of deception—to take the words and the truths of the ascended masters and of the great wisdom teachings of all time and to repeat them and to have everyone agree with you, "Why, yes, I believe that. I believe that."

The only thing that gives us a sense that she is quoting truth but she is on the left-handed path is that original point of rebellion—and, of course, the earmarks of the most recent life and her past life of her obsession with herself, her worship of herself, and the carryover of this defiance. She vows she is going to be great. And she throws in the name of Christ and God and speaks of the Gospels. But really, it is to herself she is making this vow.

We have to realize that the New Age movement today has become obsessed with self and body. It has moved into a selfish vibration where people are pursuing their own lives for their own selves. And Nin is a person who fits into that culture—absolute freedom in sex and sexuality and simply living to observe herself in living, living to observe herself doing what she is doing and then writing this down.

There were seven volumes, seven hundred pages of diaries that she wrote about herself in this final life. It takes an awful lot of interest in oneself to spend one's life writing about oneself when there are so many more interesting things to be doing.

I would like you to learn the lesson from this lifestream that the words of people do not tell their story. The smiles of people do not tell their story. But somehow, we are a nation that enjoys being stroked with the right words, the right smile, the right kind of people that we think that we should be associating with.

We gain a certain wellness and a certain sense of well-being from surface interactions and surface communications. It's almost as if we do not want to know that there is such a thing as an individual soul committed to the left-handed path and to Absolute Evil, by cleverly couching all of this into what is modern and what is psychoanalytic, et cetera. We see people playing upon and then preying upon many other individuals who simply are not discerning enough or deep enough themselves to know that they're not talking to someone who is leading them to God, although it seems so, but leading them in the other direction, which is nihilism.

Nin denies being narcissistic in the worship of herself. But to me, that is what she is. She is thought highly of and considered one of the most influential people of the twentieth century, especially in the feminist and women's movement.

Anaïs Nin died on January 14, 1977, and she is now on the fourteenth level of the astral plane.* So you can see that the law is just. People cannot parade around in defiance of God, misleading a generation of women without paying the price.

But what is the price? The fact of the matter is that she spent lifetimes in the darkness of the astral plane. You can be in the astral plane in physical embodiment. The astral plane is a state of consciousness. That is where she created her books and her writings. That is where she lived her life. And so she is in death as she was in life, in that same state of consciousness.

*The astral plane is one of the four planes of Matter. It is the repository of the collective thought/feeling patterns, conscious and unconscious, of mankind. The pristine purpose of this plane is the amplification of the pure thoughts and feelings of God in man. Instead, it has been polluted with the negative emotions of man. The astral plane includes what the Catholic Church has called purgatory and hell. It has thirty-three levels in descending order of density.

CHAPTER 5

# The Use and Misuse of Power

---

LIFE NUMBER 1: Place: Atlantis
Date: c. 10,400 BC
Sex: Male

It was the time of decline on Atlantis. The continent had split into six provinces. Cities were decaying. Parts were overgrown and unsafe to enter. Guerrilla bands controlled sections of the provinces. Industrial plants sat idle and were falling apart. Vestiges of representative government remained, but real power lay in various military leaders.

This person incarnated as the first son in a military family. His father was the soul who would later incarnate as Joseph Stalin. As son, he organized a military takeover of the largest province. He disbanded the elected government. Although he promised to improve conditions, he created a totalitarian state. He set up prison camps for the indigent or indolent.

He drove farmers from their land under the pretext that the government could work the land more efficiently with larger equipment. This uprooted people who moved to the cities. The province ended up a dictatorship, with wealth concentrated in the hands of the few. Classes were divided into the very rich and the very poor. A new serf class arose. It was a dismal time. He died after ruling for 30 years.

---

**LIFE NUMBER 2:** Place: Atlantis
Sex: Male

He was reborn in one of his own slave labor camps on Atlantis. He died at age 10.

---

**LIFE NUMBER 3:** Place: Ancient Egypt
Sex: Male

He was a slave working on building a pyramid in Egypt (not the Pyramids at Giza). Nikita Khrushchev and Joseph Stalin were his bosses. He was rewarded by them for being the hardest-working slave and put in a position as foreman.

He rose rapidly through the ranks as a capable administrator. He knew how to give the right combination of encouragement and the lash. He listened to other people's problems. He was poisoned by Khrushchev, who was jealous that he was gaining too much power. He died of this poisoning.

---

**LIFE NUMBER 4:** Place: Ancient Greece
Sex: Male

He was born into a noble family in ancient Greece. He became skilled in debate. He learned to sway popular opinion. He contributed to the downfall of Greece. He was cruel to slaves. He caused some to have their legs tied together at the knees for punishment. Six of them later became cripples and had to beg for a living. He had a wife but no children.

---

**LIFE NUMBER 5:** Place: North Africa
Date: 900 AD
Sex: Male

He was a black slave in a Muslim state in North Africa in 900 AD. He worked in the fields during the first part of his life. He was castrated by his owner. Nevertheless, he loved a beautiful slave girl.

In later life, a cart went out of control and knocked him over. The wheels ran over his legs at the knee and he could never walk again. His master was kind and took care of him until he died.

---

**LIFE NUMBER 6:** Place: Denmark
Date: Twelfth century
Sex: Female

Her name is Teka. She lived in Denmark in the twelfth century. Her husband was a fisherman. She spent a devoted life caring for his nets. They had ten children. During middle age, she was active in community affairs and organizing a system of preparing for and responding to storms. In old age, she was shipwrecked and rescued but died soon after.

---

**LIFE NUMBER 7:** Place: Britain
Date: 1789 to 1814
Sex: Female

She was a young girl of noble family in Britain. She died of tuberculosis in 1814 at age 25. She had no husband or children.

---

**LIFE NUMBER 8:** Place: America
Date: 1824 to 1878
Sex: Male

He was born to a New York banking family in 1824. He was involved in efforts to establish a central bank apart from the government. He was involved in the efforts to begin the Civil War for the purposes of greater profits. He was killed by a runaway horse carriage in the streets of New York.

Franklin Delano Roosevelt (1882–1945)

**LIFE NUMBER 9:** Place: America
Date: 1882 to 1945
Sex: Male

Franklin Delano Roosevelt was born into a wealthy, politically powerful and socially prominent family on January 30, 1882. He was the only child of his father's second marriage. The Roosevelts had been in the country since the seventeenth century. Their wealth came from a sugar refinery and real estate. By the time Franklin was born, his father, James, was a prominent member of New York society. His mother's father had become wealthy through opium trade with China.

Franklin attended Harvard and married his distant cousin Eleanor Roosevelt in 1905. He was elected to the state Senate in 1910 and reelected in 1912. Between 1913 and 1920, he served as Assistant Secretary of the Navy under Woodrow Wilson.

In 1917, Eleanor discovered that he was having an affair with Lucy Mercer, her former social secretary. Lucy supplied Franklin with the lively companionship that was missing in his relationship with Eleanor. Elliott Roosevelt later recalled that his parents enjoyed very few light moments: "They never enjoyed *anything* in the way of lightheartedness in their lives."[1] Eleanor offered Franklin a divorce, but he instead broke off the affair. Although they resumed their marriage, Eleanor was deeply hurt and their lives were never the same. Elliott referred to their marriage after the affair as a "partnership arrangement."

In 1921, Roosevelt was stricken with polio and was paralyzed from the waist down. You recall in that past life in ancient Greece his having injured those slaves by binding them at the knees. We always come back to pay our debts. The more you see these lifetimes, the more you realize that not one jot or tittle of the law passes away until we fulfill that law of karma.

Eleanor and Franklin Roosevelt, August 1932

## The New Deal

In 1924, he resumed his legal career and reentered public life. In 1928, he was elected governor of New York. In 1932, when America was in the depths of the Great Depression, he received the Democratic nomination for president. He campaigned on a platform of "relief, recovery and reform." As soon as he was sworn in, Roosevelt called Congress into a special session, and in "100 Days" they passed the massive, far-reaching legislation known as the New Deal.

From 1933 to 1945, he served as the 32nd president of the United States. When he took office, thirteen million people were unemployed and the banking system was on the verge of collapse. Millions heard his confident words over the radio: "The only thing we have to fear is fear itself."

He was able to galvanize the public behind his reforms with his informal and relaxed "fireside chats" over the radio. His New Deal legislation was passed with lightning speed. It included the creation of numerous federal agencies such as the Federal

Deposit Insurance Corporation and the Public Works Administration. He put people back to work, and they were grateful.

However, in 1935 and 1936 the Supreme Court declared some New Deal legislation unconstitutional. Roosevelt proposed adding new justices to the court. Many people felt that he was simply trying to pack the Court and undermine its separation-of-powers function. Roosevelt met with his first major legislative defeat.

The legacy of the New Deal has been hotly debated almost since it was enacted. On the positive side, it gave people hope in one of America's darkest hours. In the short run, it addressed some of the acute problems of unemployment. But it had negative consequences as well. First, it was not an effective economic program. By 1937, the economy was still in the doldrums. And many of the structural economic and social problems we have today can be traced, at least in part, to New Deal policies.

For example, in 1933, Roosevelt effectively took the nation off the gold standard. That enabled politicians and bankers to manipulate the economy through monetary and fiscal policy. If we had the economic discipline of the gold standard, we would not have a deficit problem of the magnitude we have today.[2]

The New Deal vastly increased the power of the federal bureaucracy. Tax-and-spend liberalism took firm hold during the Roosevelt years. Today, it is widely recognized that the federal government is often the problem rather than the solution. Most people recognize the need for some kind of social welfare assistance, but they also recognize that many government programs are simply out of control. While the failure of government programs today cannot all be laid at the feet of Roosevelt, they had their roots in New Deal legislation.

After World War II began, Roosevelt built up American strength and made the country into the "arsenal of democracy." He led the nation victoriously through World War II.

Churchill, Roosevelt and Stalin at Yalta, 1945

## Roosevelt and Stalin

One of the key relationships of Roosevelt's life was his relationship with Joseph Stalin. Most historians agree that he completely misjudged Stalin. During the war, he attempted to befriend Stalin. He bent over backwards to convince Stalin that he could trust the West. As Roosevelt's adviser Averell Harriman later wrote: "He was determined, establishing a close personal relationship with Stalin in wartime, to build confidence among the Kremlin leaders that Russia, now an acknowledged major power, could trust the West."[3]

George Kennan, one of America's foremost modern diplomats, wrote:

> I also have in mind FDR's evident conviction that Stalin, while perhaps a somewhat difficult customer, was only, after all, a person like any other person; that the reason we hadn't been able to get along with him in the past was that we had never really had anyone with the proper personality and the proper qualities of sympathy and imagination to deal with him... and that if only he could be exposed to the persuasive charms of someone like FDR himself,

> ideological preconceptions would melt and Stalin's co-operation with the West could easily be arranged. For these assumptions there were no grounds whatsoever; and they were of a puerility unworthy of a statesman of FDR's stature.[4]

Roosevelt told his longtime friend William Bullitt: "I think if I give him [Stalin] everything I possibly can, and ask nothing from him in return, *noblesse oblige,* he won't try to annex anything and will work with me for a world of peace and democracy."[5]

Roosevelt made many concessions to Stalin throughout the war. At a conference held in Yalta in February 1945, he gave the Soviet Union territories in Japan and China in exchange for Stalin's agreement to enter the war against Japan. The decisions at Yalta permitted the creation of Soviet-style governments in Poland, Czechoslovakia, Yugoslavia, Hungary, Romania and Bulgaria. Stalin agreed to "free and unfettered" elections in Poland as early as possible. After the war, free elections never happened in Poland and the Soviet puppet government remained in power.

Winston Churchill and Roosevelt had greatly differing views of the postwar future of Europe. Churchill's private dream was to establish a United States of Europe, excluding the Soviet Union, in which "the barriers between nations will be greatly minimized and unrestricted travel will be possible."[6] Roosevelt, on the other hand, in a conversation with Francis Cardinal Spellman, revealed that he had no compunctions about abandoning Europe to Stalin. He said that the European people would simply have to "endure Russian domination in the hope that—in ten or twenty years—the European influence would bring the Russians to become less barbarous."[7] Roosevelt here revealed himself an elitist to the core.

Privately, Churchill opposed the Yalta agreement, the Declaration on Liberated Europe. But he supported it publicly so as not to endanger his alliance with America.

Another example of Roosevelt's mad pursuit of friendship with Stalin was his refusal to press Stalin to help the Poles. This was at a time when the Polish Home Army was being slaughtered by the Germans while Stalin's Red Army sat on the other side of the Vistula River and watched. Kennan wrote of Roosevelt's attitude toward Poland: "One gets the impression that it seemed to him of little importance whether these areas were Polish or Russian. His anxiety was rather that he had a large body of voting constituents in this country of Polish or Baltic origin."[8]

Roosevelt saw greater danger in British imperialism than Soviet imperialism, despite the fact that the Soviets had recently slaughtered millions of their own people. Whose side was he really on, anyway?

Even when the Soviets violated the Yalta agreements in the spring of 1945, Roosevelt continued to court Stalin. You can see these relationships were formed a long time ago and there was the absolute need of FDR to have that father figure and to please that father figure. Millions of Americans lost their lives for the liberation of Europe. And at the end of the war, the Soviets were handed Eastern Europe by a treaty that Churchill didn't want, but that Roosevelt forced on him and that Stalin lapped up.

This is a very serious karma—the karma of one individual who caused the enslavement of the nations of Eastern Europe. For decades these people were under the tyrannical rule of secret police and the armies of the USSR—because one man had this bent in his personality.

This is when you begin to ask yourself, who is FDR? Where did he come from? And how could one man so distort the flame of freedom and the flame of liberty for so many millions of people for so long?

Roosevelt died of a massive cerebral hemorrhage on April 12, 1945. I am not at liberty to tell you where he is now.

CHAPTER 6

# Tests Passed and Karma Balanced

---

**LIFE NUMBER 1:** Place: Atlantis
Sex: Male

He lived in the very distant past when Atlantean tribes were first uniting to form a collective government. He was a leader who organized four tribes to fight together and establish a joint government. The coalition fell apart when he demanded one of the wives of the other leaders. When the leader refused, he took that wife anyway. War resulted.

This is how the abduction took place. He sent a picked band of men to abduct her from her tent one night. The men killed six guards, creeping up through the dust and slitting their throats with sharp stone knives. Later, the war went against his tribe. In an outburst of anger at him for his folly, the tribe sacrificed both him and his new wife to the gods. Each was tied separately on a platform of wood. Their stomachs were sliced open. They were left to have their organs eaten by birds until they perished.

---

**LIFE NUMBER 2:** Place: Atlantis
Date: c. 10,900 BC
Sex: Male

Again he became a military leader on Atlantis. It was some time after Phylos the Tibetan's embodiment as Zailm Numinos, for those familiar with his story.[1] He was a member of the military council responsible for the nation of Atlantis. Tribes from the north were threatening one of Atlantis' most prosperous provinces. This leader favored negotiation and tried to work out a settlement with the tribes.

It was a time of economic difficulty and civic strife, and so his settlement was popular because troops would not have to be committed to defend the province. When the tribes invaded the province, slaughtered every man in the capital city and took the women and children as slaves, this man was devastated.

He resigned from office. He was deserted by everyone—friends, wife and children. He ended up committing suicide. He threw himself off a white marble bridge into one of the capital city's narrow ravines. It was rocky with a shallow stream at the bottom. He was killed instantly.

---

**LIFE NUMBER 3:** Place: Atlantis
Date: The time of its sinking
Sex: Male

He was reborn as a slave in the last days of Atlantis and was forced to perform menial labor in the fields. This was a partial paying off of his karma for the military disaster when the Atlantean province was invaded by the northern tribes. He was taken by his master to the American continent to watch over his affairs there. The master returned to Atlantis, leaving him in charge of a mining operation.

Soon after, the Atlantean continent sank. Thus he was one of the few Atlanteans to survive the sinking of the continent. After Atlantis sank, he helped to organize a primitive government among the survivors. He lived to an honorable age and was respected for his ideas. In middle age he met his twin flame, but she was married to someone else. She acknowledged him but stayed with her husband. He never married.

---

**LIFE NUMBER 4:** Place: South America
Date: Ancient
Sex: Female

She was abducted from her father's home in an ancient civilization in South America. A rival tribe forced her to serve as a prostitute when she was young. When she grew older, she was sent to do menial labor in the fields. In old age, she was assigned to help care for the daughter of the king.

This was the same soul she (or he) had abducted on Atlantis. This was her opportunity to pay off some of the karma for the abduction and subsequent death of the woman on Atlantis. She gave great love and affection to this girl and developed a bond with her. She was buried with honor when she died.

---

**LIFE NUMBER 5:** Place: Southwestern United States
Date: c. 5,000 BC
Sex: Female

She belonged to a tribe that lived peacefully in the southwestern United States. Her husband was the woman she had abducted on Atlantis, her twin flame. They had a happy and productive life. She bore five children and raised them all to a healthy adulthood. She passed her test of learning to nurture and serve life.

---

**LIFE NUMBER 6:** Place: Far East
Sex: Male

He became a great warlord in the Far East. His major test was the use of power. He passed some tests and failed others. He was responsible for cruel torture and the institution of brutal punishment of criminals throughout his province. He had a favorite concubine, but he ordered her death after hearing rumors of her infidelity. He had really loved her, but he was quick to believe the rumors because he did not want to be humiliated. He ordered his men to have her head, hands and feet cut off and her body thrown to the dogs.

He accomplished some good in this life. He made a truce with other warlords and presided over an era of peace and prosperity. And he fought several brilliant battles. Before coming to power, he publicly humiliated his enemies and caused their downfall by rumor and gossip. This was karma he would have to pay off in future lives.

---

**LIFE NUMBER 7:** Place: England
Date: 1650 to 1722
Sex: Male

John Churchill, Duke of Marlborough, has been called one of the greatest military commanders in history. He was born on May 26, 1650. At age 15, he served as a page to the Duke of York, who was later crowned King James II. When Churchill was 17, he received a commission in the Foot Guards and began a successful military career. He married Sarah Jennings for love, not money. Although they eventually became extremely wealthy, they had very little money to begin with.

Churchill remained in the service of the Duke of York, carrying out confidential assignments for him and accompanying him when he was in exile. He later switched his allegiance from the Catholic James II to the Protestant William of Orange.

When James II was expelled from England and William of Orange became King William III, the new king rewarded Churchill's allegiance by making him the Earl of Marlborough. He was also given a succession of military commands in Flanders and in Ireland between 1689 and 1691, which he executed with great success. He was imprisoned for a short time in the Tower of London on suspicion of working toward the restoration of the exiled James II.

John Churchill, Duke of Marlborough

Marlborough's influence at court increased when Queen Anne came to the throne after William's death. She made him the Duke of Marlborough. The Duchess of Marlborough became a close adviser and friend of the queen. Together the Marlboroughs were a central power beside the queen.

The Duke's reputation as a military general was unrivaled until Napoleon. He was also a successful diplomat. He created and maintained the alliance of nations that opposed the French king Louis XIV. Marlborough was a Tory (a conservative) who supported the Crown, the court and the Church. As the old Tories began to leave government, the Marlboroughs advocated an alliance with the Whigs, who wanted to limit the authority of the Crown. Queen Anne strongly disliked the Whigs. The Duchess's influence on the queen diminished. The Duke was accused of misappropriating public funds and dismissed from office. They left the country and settled abroad.

When George I succeeded Queen Anne to the throne, he restored Churchill to favor. Churchill returned to England, but he no longer played an active role in public affairs. He died at Windsor on June 16, 1722.

---

**LIFE NUMBER 8:** Place: Malaya
Date: Late eighteenth and early nineteenth centuries
Sex: Male

In the late eighteenth and early nineteenth centuries in Malaya, Southeast Asia, he became an enlightened ruler, known for wise practices often exceeding the standards of his time and place. He repaid his past karma for executing his concubine. She was reincarnated as his wife and he raised her up and educated her. Later he gave her honors and wealth.

In this lifetime he also treated other slaves kindly, reduced punishments, motivated people to produce better harvests and instituted a system of fair taxation.

Can you guess who this subject was in the twentieth century?

Winston Churchill. It often happens that people have the same name in different lifetimes.

---

**LIFE NUMBER 9:** Place: England
Date: 1874 to 1965
Sex: Male

Winston Churchill lived from 1874 to 1965. There are a number of parallels with his life as the Duke of Marlborough. For example, he switched parties from Liberal to Conservative and back again, just as Marlborough switched his allegiance. Winston Churchill actually wrote a biography of Marlborough that painted him in a more favorable light than other biographies. Nothing like doing up your own past life!

Sir Winston Leonard Spencer Churchill (1874–1965)

Winston Churchill in the military uniform of a hussar in 1895, at the age of 21

Winston's father was a direct descendant of the Duke of Marlborough. His mother was an American, the daughter of a New York financier. As a young man, he served in the British Army in India and Egypt. He also worked as a correspondent in Cuba and South Africa. He wrote books on his experiences and supported himself on the income from these books.

At age 25, he was elected to Parliament as a Conservative. He lost popularity when he joined the Liberal party in 1904. Most likely, the reason he switched his allegiance was because he disagreed with the Conservative leadership's position on trade. They supported a tariff, while he believed in free trade.

In 1908, he married the beautiful Clementine Hozier. They were happily married for life. This marriage provided a stable basis for Churchill's turbulent career. They named their second daughter Sarah, after the Duke of Marlborough's wife.

Clementine Churchill, 1915

In 1911, he became First Lord of the Admiralty. He realized that Germany was planning to launch a war when it safely could. Consequently, he began to strengthen the British fleet to prepare for possible war. He was blamed for three important defeats in the war: Antwerp, the naval campaign in the Dardanelles, and Gallipoli. But it was later realized that he had not been given either the power or the logistical support to make the campaigns a success; thus many believe that he was not really to blame. Nevertheless, he resigned from government in 1915.

Churchill returned to public office as the Minister of Munitions in 1917. He greatly increased the production of war matériel and supported the development of the tank. The tank later became the weapon that broke through the stalemate of trench warfare on the Western Front. We can see him step by step undoing the karma of allowing the Atlantean province to be invaded without defense. His soul never forgot. His soul took responsibility for that failure. And this time he would do it right.

Between 1921 and 1922, Churchill served as Colonial Secretary. He helped negotiate the treaty that ended the Irish War of Independence and was involved in resolving problems in the Middle East. However, he opposed self-rule for India and Burma.

In 1924, he returned to the Conservative party. In 1925, Churchill put Great Britain back on the gold standard at the rate of exchange that had been in place before the First World War. The economy reacted violently. There was deflation, a rise in unemployment and a miners' strike. Churchill was blamed for these problems.

In 1929, the Conservatives were voted out, and Churchill spent the next ten years out of office. During this time, he perceived that Nazism in Germany, Fascism in Italy and Communism in Russia were threats to democracy. He opposed Prime Minister Neville Chamberlain's policy of disarmament and giving in to Hitler's demands.

Churchill urged military preparation, but few listened. When World War II broke out, he was appointed First Lord of the Admiralty. Chamberlain was forced to resign when Germany invaded the Low Countries. Churchill then became Prime Minister and brilliantly led Britain through the war. Thus he balanced his karma from the two debacles on Atlantis.

He had his shortcomings. He was overly bombastic at times. His inability to successfully oppose Stalin and Roosevelt at Yalta and Potsdam resulted in the enslavement of Eastern Europe. He lost friends through unwillingness to compromise and being too outspoken. But he passed the test of preferring right over popularity that he had failed on Atlantis by allowing the province to be invaded and destroyed.

He married his twin flame and paid the remainder of the karma he had for abducting her on Atlantis and causing her death.

Churchill suffered a severe stroke on January 15, 1965, and died in London nine days later, at the age of 90. He has since returned to embodiment.

CHAPTER 7

# The Iron Lady

---

**LIFE NUMBER 1:** Place: Lemuria
Sex: Female

The next person is a woman today. For her first life, we go back to Lemuria, the continent that sank beneath the Pacific Ocean. She is female. It is said that Lemuria sank about 12,500 years ago, or about a thousand years before the sinking of Atlantis.[1]

At one time she was High Priestess in the Temple of the Divine Mother on Lemuria. It was a time of religious decline. On the positive side, she convinced many people to return to worship. She focused a greater flame in Lemuria and prolonged the civilization. On the negative side, she convinced the government to institute a policy of coercion in religious worship. Peasants were forced to go to the temple, sometimes at the point of a spear.

---

**LIFE NUMBER 2:** Place: Atlantis
Sex: Male

He had the choice to pursue a career in the priesthood or in government on Atlantis. He chose government and became a prominent legislator. He advocated reform in the laws concerning slaves. He was able to make conditions better for slaves and actually instituted a ten-year process whereby a slave could free himself.

His private life was a tragedy. During middle age, he fell in love with the daughter of a fellow legislator. He arranged for his wife to be murdered by having a slave push her over a wall of the garden surrounding their house. The slave confessed to authorities out of feelings of guilt. The legislator was publicly tried and resigned in disgrace. He was exiled to a small island where he lived out his life. The slave was executed.

The wife he had ordered killed is one of this individual's children today. The slave is the other child. The young girl he was in love with was his twin flame and she (now in a female embodiment) is married to him today.

---

**LIFE NUMBER 3:** Place: Atlantis
Sex: Female

The karma for killing his wife was set aside so that he could become yet another public servant on Atlantis. This is one of the amazing acts of grace that God gives us, that the Lords of Karma give us, that life gives us. When we go before the Lords of Karma and we are penitent and desirous of atoning for our misdeeds, they will sometimes set aside karma so that we can go forth and create a positive momentum of good karma before we have to deal with the descent of the negative karma.

Good karma is like money in the bank. It's energy in your causal body (your body of light in the planes of Spirit). God has done this, I am certain, for all of us at one time or another in situations where we have sinned and then been profoundly remorseful. God has allowed us to go on and serve to set life free before coming to the time, such as this life, when we would have the violet flame and opportunity and understanding and enlightenment so that we could deal with some of the harsher realities of our karma.

This soul was given such an opportunity, and this time, he embodied as a woman on Atlantis. She became a scientist and organized and implemented a new sanitation system for the towns and cities that eliminated the need for sewer pipes. All waste was processed in the home and either used for energy or picked up by municipal garbage authorities once a month.

In private life, she never married. She had a series of affairs in early life. She was unable to develop a stable relationship with anyone because of the sad ending to her past life.

---

**LIFE NUMBER 4:** Place: Rome
Date: First century AD
Sex: Male

He was a famous Roman senator who was directly and indirectly responsible for the death of many people. In his early years, he was a soldier stationed on Crete. He raped a girl there.

As a senator, he made positive and negative contributions to society. On the positive side, he fought for the enfranchisement of more citizens. On the negative side, he compromised for the sake of politics. He threw his power with the group that lost. There was an uprising. Soldiers came out to crush it. He was exhorting the people to return home and not to revolt. However, he was still seen as a leader of the revolt.

As he exhorted the people from the second story of the house, soldiers appeared behind him and stabbed him just behind the collarbone. The lesson he learned was to be careful which party you side with and not to side with a cause you don't really believe in for the sake of politics. That is a very important lesson that we all might learn on the playground at a very early age.

In private life, he had a devoted wife and five children. They survived him. His wife was the one he had ordered to be killed before. He balanced some karma by achieving an intimate, loving relationship with her. However, he also had mistresses.

---

**LIFE NUMBER 5:** Place: Crete
Sex: Female

She embodied as a slave in Crete to pay back some of the karma incurred by raping a girl on Crete. She served as a concubine to a wealthy farmer. The farmer was the reincarnation of the girl he had raped as a Roman soldier. It is amazing to see how karma keeps on intertwining.

---

**LIFE NUMBER 6:** Place: Britain
Date: Seventeenth century
Sex: Male

He was a member of the British parliament during the English Civil War (1642 to 1648). He was on the side of Oliver Cromwell and the Parliament. He opposed King Charles I. He was one of the participants in the "Rump Parliament," which tried and condemned Charles I to death.

---

**LIFE NUMBER 7:** Place: Britain
Sex: Male

He was an oil merchant in London. He got into debt and was forced out of business by greedy competitors. He was reduced to life as a beggar. Eventually he was murdered and dumped in the Thames. His wife and children starved and died. In this life he was repaying the karma for a Roman merchant he had ordered to be ruined. The merchant begged for mercy but he had no mercy.

---

**LIFE NUMBER 8:** Place: Britain
Date: Nineteenth century
Sex: Female

She was born in England but emigrated with her parents to North Carolina during the 1840s. She became a schoolteacher. During the Civil War, she helped to organize and care for the wounded and dying. She used her money to help the sick and bereaved. Many of those she helped were those to whom she owed karmic debts from her life as a Roman senator.

She had an ill-fated romance. She met her twin flame during the war. She spent only one night with him before he was killed in battle. She never married.

It often happens that people have a very brief encounter with their twin flame in one lifetime or another. It is a mercy and a grace that is given to reestablish the heart tie, which sets the sail for them finding one another in the next life or a future time where they can be together for a greater amount of time or even a lifetime.

You can always see the mercy of the Law side by side with the justice of the Law if you look for it. Sometimes people forget to say to themselves, "It might have been much worse." Sometimes we only look at how bad things are and don't realize that, but for the grace of God, things could be much, much worse than what has happened to us in life.

---

**LIFE NUMBER 9:** Place: Britain
Date: 1925 to 2013
Sex: Female

Margaret Thatcher—so beloved by so many people and so hated by so many people—was the prime minister of Britain from 1979 to 1990.

Her father, Alfred Roberts, was the shaping influence in her life. He was a grocer—self-taught and well-read. Roberts was always dedicated to the public good. He was thrifty to the point of being parsimonious, fiercely patriotic, a devoted Methodist who preached at church. She said of him: "I owe almost everything to my father.... He taught me that you first sort out what you believe in. You then apply it. You don't compromise on things that matter."[2]

Here is an example of someone who had a wonderful relationship with a father that she could admire and respect. There is

Margaret Hilda Thatcher (1925–2013)

a book that has been written about fathers and daughters which explains how key the relationship of the father to the daughter is to her entire future, her sexuality, her sense of herself as a person. The abandoned daughter suffers almost more than the abandoned son, although the abandoned son also suffers when the father leaves the household.

No matter what it costs you as parents, make your peace at some level and stick with your children until they are mature and able to move forward. It is so very important to understand that when you bring forth life, you become responsible for that life, that soul, that psychology and how they will face the future. Children do not do well without the strong support of both parents.

Thatcher studied chemistry at Oxford. She married Denis Thatcher, a well-to-do businessman, in 1951. She began to study law and passed the bar in 1953. She had twins, Mark and Carol, in 1953. She was elected to Parliament in 1959 and held various positions in government until 1975, when she became the leader of the Conservative Party. She attacked socialism for creating a spendthrift society.

In May 1979, she became Prime Minister of Great Britain, the first woman to hold this office. Reviewers of her leadership credit her with having turned around the economy from the "wealth-consuming public sector and big unions to the wealth-creating private sector."[3] She initiated the most ambitious privatization venture in the Western world, brought union lawlessness under control, held inflation in check, and "revived the private sector by promoting market competition."[4]

She resigned in November 1990 after her popularity ratings fell to 23 percent. The primary issue was the poll tax, a flat tax on everyone regardless of income. The amount of the tax was to be decided by each local community, but local governments set the taxes much higher than expected and Thatcher was the target of the people's blame.

Denis and Margaret Thatcher, 1984

Britain was also suffering from increasing unemployment and rising inflation. Polls showed that people thought Thatcher was out of touch with the common people and that she talked down to them.

Thatcher remained a powerful force in global politics for a number of years. She was one of the few people who had the courage to say that the civil war in Yugoslavia was a moral issue and that the world had a duty to come to the aid of the Croats and the Bosnians.

Margaret Thatcher died in 2013.

CHAPTER 8

# Charles Lindbergh

*By the Editors*

> *Am I an individual, or am I an evolving life stream composed of countless selves?... As one identity, I was born in* A.D. *1902. But as* A.D. *twentieth-century man, I am billions of years old. The life I consider as myself has existed though past eons with unbroken continuity. Individuals are custodians of the life stream—temporal manifestations of far greater being, forming from and returning to their essence like so many dreams.*
>
> Charles Lindbergh

Elizabeth Clare Prophet's original plan in delivering this lecture was to discuss the past lives of nine individuals. Unfortunately, due to limitations of time, she was able to prepare and deliver her analysis of only seven of those nine.

The seventh individual was originally planned to be Charles Lindbergh, the American aviator. We have compiled this chapter based on the historical record and comments that Mark and Elizabeth Prophet

Charles Augustus Lindbergh (1902–1974)

have made on two of his past lives: the Egyptian pharaoh who enslaved the Israelites and Abraham Lincoln. These three lives in themselves present an intriguing study in karma and reincarnation.

---

**LIFE NUMBER 1:** Place: Ancient Egypt
Date: c. 1273 to c. 1203 BC
Sex: Male

Merneptah, Pharaoh of Egypt, was born around 1273 BC, the thirteenth son of Ramses II, known as Ramses the Great, and one of his queens, Isinofre.

His father lived a long life and reigned for sixty-seven years. The start of Merneptah's reign was around 1213 BC, when he was around 60 years of age. He came to power only because all his older brothers died before him. He ruled for almost ten years. It was either before or during his reign that the Israelites were enslaved in Egypt.

He successfully defended Egypt against a serious threat of invasion from Libya. He learned that the Sea Peoples had joined and armed the Libyans and were preparing to attack the administrative and religious centers of Memphis and Heliopolis from the west. After receiving assurances of military success in a dream and marshalling his forces, he met them on the battlefield. His archers massacred the foe, then the chariotry and infantry routed the enemy.

The events described in the book of Exodus occurred in Egypt in this era. The Bible does not give the name of the pharaoh whom Moses faced, and contemporary Egyptian records make no reference to the events described in the Bible, so there has been considerable disagreement regarding which pharaoh was involved. In popular culture, this pharaoh is generally thought of as Ramses, since this is what was portrayed in Cecil B. de Mille's epic *The Ten Commandments* and in the 1998 animated film *Prince of Egypt.* Isaac Asimov, in his *Guide to the Bible,* makes the case that Merneptah was the pharaoh of the exodus, and this was what Mark Prophet said, having seen the mummy of Merneptah in an Egyptian museum.

Funerary figurine depicting the Pharaoh Merneptah

According to the biblical account, before the time of Moses' birth (when Merneptah's father, Ramses II, or grandfather, Seti I, was pharaoh), the pharaoh realized that the Israelites had become so numerous that they had become a threat to the security of Egypt. The Israelites had been residing in the Nile Delta region since the time of Joseph, some four hundred years earlier.

Exodus 1:10–11 records Pharaoh's concern that the Israelites might join with Egypt's enemies and take up arms against Egypt. "Accordingly," states Exodus, "they put slave drivers over the Israelites to wear them down under heavy loads. In this way they built the store-cities of Pithom and Rameses." When the Israelites continued to multiply, Pharaoh gave the order to have all Hebrew boys thrown into the river.[1]

Jewish historian Josephus, writing in the second century AD

in his *Antiquities of the Jews*, tells a somewhat different version of the story. He said that one of the sacred scribes of Egypt told the pharaoh that a child born to the Israelites would bring down Egyptian domination, raise up the Israelites, and in so doing, would obtain glory.[2]

The Bible records that baby Moses was hidden by his Hebrew mother along the river Nile. The daughter of Pharaoh found the boy and raised the child as her own in the royal court. He would therefore likely have grown up with Merneptah as a close relative.

According to the Bible, Moses "was learned in all the wisdom of the Egyptians, and was mighty in words and in deeds."[3] He lived as an Egyptian of princely rank until he was about 40 years old,[4] when Exodus records that he "went out unto his brethren, and looked on their burdens: and he spied an Egyptian smiting an Hebrew, one of his brethren. And he looked this way and that way, and when he saw that there was no man, he slew the Egyptian, and hid him in the sand."[5]

In this, Moses' first act of public record, he took the law into his own hands and for the first time allowed his sympathy for the Hebrews to be known. He fled Egypt to the land of Midian, where he lived for another 40 years. The Bible tells us that it was in Midian that "the angel of the LORD appeared unto him in a flame of fire out of the midst of a bush: he looked, and behold, the bush burned with fire, and the bush was not consumed."

The LORD said to Moses, "I have surely seen the affliction of my people in Egypt, have heard their cry.... I know their sorrows." Then he commanded Moses: "Come now therefore, and I will send thee unto Pharaoh, that thou mayest bring forth my people the children of Israel out of Egypt."[6]

At the age of 80, Moses went back to the court of Pharaoh to demand that he allow the Israelites to journey three days into the wilderness to make a sacrifice. Pharaoh refused. Instead, he increased their workload, requiring them to harvest stubble in the fields instead of being supplied with straw for their brick making, while still producing the same amount of bricks. This is the origin of the phrase "making bricks without straw."

Moses returned to Pharaoh to make the same demand: "Let my people go!" His brother, Aaron, accompanied him, and as proof of divine favor for their cause, Aaron cast his rod down on the ground and it turned into a serpent. The Egyptian court magicians duplicated this feat, but Aaron's rod swallowed up those produced by the court magicians. Despite this demonstration, Pharaoh refused to let the Israelites leave.

There followed ten plagues upon the land of Egypt. All the waters of Egypt turned to blood. There was a plague of frogs, then a plague of lice or gnats. The Egyptians' livestock suffered diseases, the Egyptian people suffered from a plague of boils, there was a rain of fiery hail and a plague of locusts. Several times Pharaoh promised to let the Israelites go if Moses removed the plague, but each time when the plague was removed, he refused to honor his promise.

The ninth plague was three days of darkness. This time Pharaoh offered to let the Israelites go but without their livestock. When Moses would not agree to this, Pharaoh said he would have Moses killed if he came into his presence again. Moses then announced the tenth and most terrible plague—the death of the firstborn of every man and beast in the land, including the firstborn of Pharaoh himself. Moses told the Israelites to mark their lintels and doorposts with the blood of a lamb and to celebrate a special meal, including unleavened bread, that the angel of death might "pass over" their households and that their firstborn would be spared.

After this plague, Pharaoh ordered the Israelites to leave Egypt. However, even now, Pharaoh had a change of heart. He set out with chariots to pursue the Israelites and bring them back to Egypt. When it appeared that the Israelites were trapped between Pharaoh's army and the Red Sea, Moses parted the waters to allow his people to pass through. When Pharaoh's army attempted to follow, the waters returned and they were drowned. Thus the Israelites escaped, but because of their unbelief, they had to wander in the wilderness for forty years before entering the Promised Land.

Merneptah is thought to have survived when his army was drowned in pursuing the Israelites and died around 1203 BC.

On a number of occasions in the account in Exodus, it is said that God "hardened the heart" of Pharaoh so that he would not let the Israelites go. It has always been a puzzle to students of the Bible as to why God would do this, causing Pharaoh to make choices that would cause so much seemingly unnecessary suffering for the people of Egypt.

The answer lies in karma. The hardening of the heart represents the accelerated return of karma. Cycles had turned to the point where the karma of Pharaoh had come due—and evidently also the karma of his people. Some of this karma may have been for the enslavement of the Israelites and their decades of suffering under the Egyptian taskmasters. The death of the firstborn throughout Egypt mirrors the slaughter of the male children of the Israelites at the time of Moses' birth. There may have also been a group or national karma between the Israelites and the Egyptians that extended back to Atlantis or before.

For whatever reason, this karma had come due, and it was not set aside through grace or mercy. Pharaoh had a choice as to what he would do when faced with his returning karma. He could have chosen to extend mercy, and then mercy might have also been extended to Egypt. But as often happens when dealing with returning momentums of karma, he chose to follow the old course and create more karma in the same mold rather than balance the karma by taking a higher way.

In such a case, the hope for the soul is that pride and anger might be broken by the experience of that karma outplaying without mitigation. Karma becomes the instructor of the soul when people no longer heed the teachers and prophets that God has sent to deliver them from their karma.

---

| **LIFE NUMBER 2:** | Place: | America |
|---|---|---|
| | Date: | 1809 to 1865 |
| | Sex: | Male |

Abraham Lincoln, "Honest Abe," was the sixteenth President of the United States of America. He was born February 12, 1809, in a log cabin in the backwoods of Kentucky. His parents were poverty-stricken and almost completely illiterate. His father, Thomas Lincoln, was a migratory carpenter and farmer descended from a weaver's apprentice who had migrated from England to Massachusetts in 1637. Little is known about Lincoln's mother, Nancy Hanks. She died in 1818 shortly after her family moved to Indiana.

Abraham was nine years old when his mother died. His father soon remarried. His stepmother, Sarah Bush Johnston, was a widow with two children of her own but she was especially fond of Abraham. Lincoln later referred to her as his "angel mother."

Abraham received less than a year of formal schooling. He taught himself by reading and rereading a small selection of books, including *Life and Memorable Actions of George Washington, Robinson Crusoe, Pilgrim's Progress* and *Aesop's Fables.* The Bible was probably the only book his family owned. Neighbors recalled how he traveled for miles to borrow a book. Lincoln said that his early surroundings provided "absolutely nothing to excite ambition for education."[7]

The Lincoln family migrated to Illinois in 1830. Abraham worked as a rail splitter and helped to clear and fence his father's new farm. At age 21, Lincoln was 6'4"—very tall for that time—physically strong, and especially skillful in wielding an ax.

He was also noted for his great strength of character. "He spoke with a backwoods twang and walked in the long-striding, flat-footed, cautious manner of a plowman. Good-natured though somewhat moody, talented as a mimic and storyteller, he readily attracted friends."[8]

Lincoln had no desire to remain a farmer. In 1831, he settled in the village of New Salem, Illinois, and tried a number of occupations: storekeeper, surveyor and village postmaster. In 1832, he enlisted as a volunteer in the Black Hawk War and was elected captain of his company.

In 1834, Lincoln was elected to the state legislature, serving four successive terms until 1841. While in the legislature he demonstrated that although he was opposed to slavery, he was not an abolitionist. Like Thomas Jefferson and the other founding fathers, he felt that slavery should be contained but not directly attacked.

Abraham Lincoln, 1863

## Personal Life

Around this time Lincoln fell in deeply in love with Ann Rutledge, and he was planning to marry her. She died of typhoid fever in August 1835, when Lincoln was away from town, an event which plunged Lincoln into a deep depression.

In 1836, Lincoln obtained his attorney's license and the following year he moved to Springfield, Illinois, where his law practice grew steadily. Within twenty years, Lincoln was one of the most successful lawyers in Illinois. He was known for his intelligence and common sense, which enabled him to go straight to the essential issues of a legal case, and also for his total honesty and sense of justice.

While he was in Springfield, Lincoln began a courtship with Mary Todd. Mary was intelligent and well-educated. She came from a distinguished Kentucky family, and some of her relatives frowned on the association. Lincoln himself had reservations about the relationship, and at one point broke their engagement. Finally the two were reconciled, and they married on November 4, 1842.

Mary gave birth to four sons. Edward died at the age of four. William died at the age of 11 while Lincoln was in the White House. Robert and Thomas outlived their father; Thomas was his father's favorite.

Lincoln, however, never forgot Ann Rutledge. He credited her as the one who motivated him to embark on his law career. One time he found a picture in a photo gallery of a girl that looked just like Ann Rutledge as he remembered her. He bought the picture and brought it home to show Mary, who got so angry that she picked up a butcher knife and tried to stab him. In spite of this, he kept that photo in the family album for many years, and every time they sat down and looked at those family photos and they would turn to that page, there would be a big argument in the room.

Mary Todd Lincoln

Ten years later, Lincoln was elected president, and he and Mary were going through their things and deciding what they would take with them to Washington, D.C. They came to the photo album, and they were looking through the pictures. When they came to the page with the picture of Ann, Lincoln said, "Molly, she meant a lot to me one time. But you've taken her place."[9] And he threw the picture on the floor.

## The Civil War

In the meantime, Lincoln's career moved forward. He served one term in Congress from 1847 to 1849. In 1856, he became a Republican and was noticed as a moderate opponent of slavery who could appeal to a broad constituency. In 1858, Lincoln was nominated by the Republican Party to oppose Stephen A. Douglas in the Illinois senate race. In his acceptance speech, he delivered the much-quoted statement: "A house divided against itself cannot stand. I believe the government cannot endure permanently half slave and half free."

In a series of debates with Douglas, he masterfully argued for the Union and the democratic ideal. Lincoln failed to win the senate seat, but the debates gained him national recognition.

In 1860, Lincoln was nominated as candidate for president at the Republican convention in Chicago. He was one of four candidates for the office of president and was elected with a minority of the popular vote but a decisive majority in the Electoral College. Lincoln's election was the signal for southern secession. By the time Lincoln had been inaugurated, seven states had seceded from the Union to form the Confederate States of America.

Lincoln's aim was to preserve the Union. In order to do this, he felt he had to take a stand against the Confederacy. Lincoln immediately summoned the militia. This precipitated the secession of four more southern states. He ordered a blockade of Confederate ports and suspended habeas corpus. He adhered to this last action in spite of much criticism and a Supreme Court ruling against him.

During the course of the war, Lincoln extended his executive powers but generally was restrained in the exercising of those powers. He was often opposed by men from his own side. Radical abolitionists criticized him for being too mild. Conservatives were skeptical that the war would be successful.

There were a number of reasons why Lincoln did not advocate an abolitionist policy. He had been elected on a platform pledging no interference with slavery. He also doubted the constitutionality of federal action to abolish slavery. He was concerned about how to incorporate four million freed Blacks into the nation's social and political life. He also wanted to keep the border slave states in the Union and feared an abolitionist program would throw them to the Confederacy.

Lincoln visiting the Union camp at Sharpsburg, Maryland, October 3, 1862

In 1862, he said: "My paramount object in this struggle is to save the Union, and is not either to save or to destroy slavery. If I could save the Union without freeing any slave, I would do it; and if I could save it by freeing all the slaves, I would do it; and if I could save it by freeing some and leaving others alone, I would also do that."[10]

On January 1, 1863, Lincoln issued the Emancipation Proclamation. It applied only to states under Confederate control, not the loyal slave states or the federally occupied areas of the Confederacy. The decree brought freedom during the war to less than 200,000 slaves, but it had enormous symbolic significance, partly because it attracted increased support for the Union cause from liberals in England and France.

Lincoln delivered the Gettysburg Address on November 19, 1863, at the dedication of the soldiers' cemetery at Gettysburg. He expressed his sorrow for the necessity of war, and his speech is considered one of the greatest public speeches ever made.

> Four score and seven years ago our fathers brought forth on this continent a new nation, conceived in liberty, and dedicated to the proposition that all men are created equal.... We here highly resolve that these dead shall not have died in vain—that this nation, under God, shall have a new birth of freedom—and that government of the people, by the people, for the people, shall not perish from the earth.

In 1864, Lincoln was reelected president by a great majority, and in his second inaugural address he set forth an eloquent explanation of karma as it pertained to the war:

> The Almighty has His own purposes. "Woe unto the world because of offenses; for it must needs be that offenses come, but woe to that man by whom the offense cometh." If we shall suppose that American slavery is one of those offenses which, in the providence of God, must needs come, but which, having continued through His appointed time, He now wills to remove, and that He gives to both North and South this terrible war as the woe due to those by whom the offense came, shall we discern therein any departure from those divine attributes which the believers in a living God always ascribe to Him? Fondly do we hope, fervently do we pray, that this mighty scourge of war may speedily pass away. Yet, if God wills that it continue until all the wealth piled by the bondsman's two hundred and fifty years of unrequited toil shall be sunk, and until every drop of blood drawn with the lash shall be paid by another drawn with the sword, as was said three thousand years ago, so still it must be said "the judgments of the Lord are true and righteous altogether."

Lincoln ended his speech with a call to forgiveness and reconciliation:

Lincoln's second inaugural address, March 4, 1865

> With malice toward none, with charity for all, with firmness in the right as God gives us to see the right, let us strive on to finish the work we are in, to bind up the nation's wounds, to care for him who shall have borne the battle and for his widow and his orphan, to do all which may achieve and cherish a just and lasting peace among ourselves and with all nations.

This was in stark contrast to the forced reparations and military occupation of the South that some in the North advocated. It seems that his heart was no longer hardened, as it had been when he was Pharaoh, and his advocacy of reconciliation rather than retribution was foundational in healing the deep wounds in the nation that had been created by the war.

Lincoln played a key role in securing the adoption of the Thirteenth Amendment to the United States' Constitution, which abolished slavery. There must have been remorse for his actions in keeping the Israelites in ancient Egypt enslaved, followed by a great desire to undo this karma in subsequent lives. And so, after more than three thousand years, the opportunity to free a people who had been enslaved came again. His karma decreed that he had to become president because only as a ruler could he actually expiate such a karma.

## A National Tragedy

On April 14, 1865, while attending an evening performance at Ford's Theater in Washington, Lincoln was shot by actor John Wilkes Booth. He died early the next morning at the age of 56. The assassination occurred on Good Friday, just days after Lee's surrender to Grant at Appomattox Court House. It was a shocking blow to the nation. Even opponents mourned his death. Later generations of Americans considered him a hero and martyr.

Elizabeth Clare Prophet has pointed out that Booth was not a lone actor in the death of Lincoln, but the agent of a much larger conspiracy:

---

Lincoln was opposed not only by the Confederacy but also by Northerners who wanted to trade with the South. Lincoln's blockade of Southern ports hurt Northern moneyed interests who had been making it rich off the war. A coalition of speculators, financiers and a group of congressmen known as the Radical Republicans determined to do anything they could to restore trade—and thus their profits. Lincoln's blockade was also slowly strangling the South. And so, in this matter the Northern bankers had a common interest with Southern Confederate leaders, businessmen and bankers.

Lincoln opposed the financial powers in other ways, as well. At the beginning of the war, Lincoln tried to borrow money from national and international bankers to finance the Union Army.

According to one source, they wanted to charge him 24 to 36 percent interest.[11] Rather than accept the bankers' terms, he decided to print paper money—greenbacks—which became legal tender. Had Lincoln borrowed money at those usurious rates, the bankers would have essentially owned the United States government at the close of the war.

Next, the bankers proposed a national banking system which would allow them to issue bank notes backed by U.S. government bonds. These notes would be just short of legal tender since the law said that they could be used in payment for all debts except duties on imports. The National Bank Act which incorporated their plan would allow expansion of the money supply through a fractional reserve system: banks could lend out more money than they had on deposit.[12]

After heavy lobbying by bankers led by Jay and Henry Cooke, the act was passed in 1863 and it resulted in a surge of inflation. Furthermore, as economist Murray Rothbard writes, it also "paved the way for the Federal Reserve System by instituting a quasi-central banking type of monetary system."[13]

An undocumented source says that during his second term in office, Lincoln planned to repeal the National Bank Act or restrict the powers it had granted bankers. Had Lincoln repealed this privilege, banks would have lost a huge money-making opportunity.

In their book *The Lincoln Conspiracy,* David Balsiger and Charles E. Sellier, Jr., demonstrate that bankers and politicians North and South plotted to eliminate Lincoln. The authors worked from the missing pages of John Wilkes Booth's diary and recently uncovered letters and documents to show that the plot against Lincoln included not only the frustrated racist John Wilkes Booth, but also Edwin Stanton, Lincoln's Secretary of War, who coveted the presidency, and greedy bankers who wanted Lincoln out of their way.

Edwin Stanton, Lincoln's Secretary of War (left), and Thurlow Weed, a New York political boss, two of the conspirators in Lincoln's assassination

Booth talked with financier Judah Benjamin, a Confederate cabinet minister who took him to meet the president of the Confederacy, Jefferson Davis. Davis arranged funds for Booth to conduct trade for the Confederacy and Benjamin arranged for him to meet with important Northern speculators, including Philadelphia financier Jay Cooke.

Cooke invited Booth to a meeting at Astor House in New York. There he met gold and cotton speculators, bankers and industrialists. Among them were Cooke's brother Henry, political boss Thurlow Weed, cotton broker Samuel Noble and the Radical Republican senator Zachariah Chandler.

Balsiger and Sellier point out that for Booth this was a curious situation—"one of the top men in the Confederacy's cabinet had sent him to meet the very bankers who financed Lincoln's war." Booth was dedicated to the victory of the Confederacy and could not understand why important figures from opposing camps were cooperating.

At the meeting Jay Cooke declared, "I will continue to have dealings with the Confederacy. Not out of fear of betrayal, but because, in peace and in war, a businessman must do business, whatever the stakes." At the end of the meeting Cooke told

Booth, "There are millions of dollars in profits to be made, and we're being denied our share. We'll be ruined if Lincoln's policies are continued."[14]

The leaders of this alliance, both North and South, hired Booth to kidnap President Lincoln, write Balsiger and Sellier. After failing in six attempts, Booth became desperate and on the night of April 14, 1865, shot the president as he sat with Mrs. Lincoln in the balcony of Ford's Theater.

The country has never been the same.[15]

---

## Lincoln's Spiritual Life

Lincoln was not particularly religious. He attended Presbyterian services with his wife, but never joined any church. He once explained: "When any church will inscribe over its altar, as its sole qualification for membership, the Saviour's condensed statement of the substance of both Law and Gospel, 'Thou shalt love the Lord thy God with all thy heart, and with all thy soul, and with all they mind, and thy neighbor, as thyself,' that church will I join with all my heart and all my soul."[16]

Throughout his life he believed in dreams and other signs and portents. As he grew older, his religious sense deepened. He saw himself as an "instrument of Providence." In 1862, he wrote: "In the present civil war it is quite possible that God's purpose is something different from the purpose of either party—and yet the human instrumentalities, working just as they do, are of the best adaptation to effect His purpose."[17]

On one occasion when she visited the Lincoln Memorial, Elizabeth Clare Prophet commented that just as Jesus knew that it was the requirement that he lay down his life, Lincoln also knew on the inner that it was the requirement for him to lay down his life for the Union. He knew that he was called to make the ultimate sacrifice, and he consented to do this.

**LIFE NUMBER 3:** Place: America
Date: 1902 to 1974
Sex: Male

Charles Lindbergh—nicknamed Slim, Lucky Lindy and the Lone Eagle—was one of the great American heroes of the early twentieth century.

Lindberg's father, Charles, was born in Stockholm, Sweden, in 1860. In the same year, Lindbergh's grandfather Ola Manson migrated to America with his family, changing his name to Lindbergh. He was a member of the Swedish parliament and had been Secretary to the King. They settled near Sauk Center, Minnesota, took up a homestead, and built their first house, a log cabin. Lindbergh's father graduated from the law school at the University of Michigan and began his practice in Little Falls, Minnesota, where he served as county attorney.

Charles Augustus Lindbergh was born on February 4, 1902, in Detroit, Michigan. In 1906, his father was elected to the U.S. Congress representing the sixth district of Minnesota, serving for ten years. Throughout his political career, he fought against the power and manipulation of the big banks. In 1917 he sought the Republican nomination to the Senate from Minnesota, running on a strongly anti-war platform, but lost the race.

His parents' marriage was not a happy one, and they parted when he was 14. He was a lonely child, emotionally split in his loyalties to his parents.

After graduating from high school, Lindbergh took a course in mechanical engineering, and two years later he entered the College of Engineering of the University of Wisconsin at Madison, where he became intensely interested in aviation. He left the University after only a year and a half to take a flying course. He nearly completed his training, but did not have the necessary bond to cover possible damage to the plane during a solo flight. He went "barnstorming" with some other pilots and also did some wing-walking and parachute jumping.

In March 1924, Lindbergh began one year of Army Air Service training, the first six months at Brooks Field, Texas, the second six months at Kelly Field, Texas. The standards were very high, and of the initial class of 104, only 18 graduated. Lindbergh was top of the class. He was commissioned Second Lieutenant in the Army Air Service Reserve.

## New York to Paris

In 1919, Raymond Orteig, a New York hotel owner, had offered a $25,000 prize for the first non-stop flight between New York and Paris. In September 1926, Lindbergh started thinking about the possibility of such a flight, and almost immediately he began to draw up plans and raise the necessary financial backing.

In February 1927, several groups and aircraft designers announced they were planning high-profile attempts, including one group led by Commander Richard E. Byrd. All of these groups were well-financed and planned to use large multi-engine aircraft with highly experienced crews. Lindbergh, with limited experience and virtually unknown to the world, planned a solo flight on a shoestring budget, and Ryan Aircraft Co., out of San Diego, offered to build a light, single-engine plane for the flight at a cost of $10,580.

In April 1927, three other planes intending to attempt the flight crashed during test flights; the crew of one plane was killed. Lindbergh completed test flights of his plane on May 4. On May 8, a French plane left Paris but never reached New York, its fate unknown. The American ambassador to France suggested that it would be an insult to the French for an American to attempt the flight so soon after their failure. There were also attempts by outsiders to persuade Lindbergh and his backers to give up because of the dangers of the flight. Undeterred, Lindbergh left New York on May 20 in *The Spirit of St. Louis,* landing in Paris 33½ hours later.

Lindbergh at Lambert Field, St. Louis, Missouri, 1923

Lindbergh's flight captured the imagination of people all over the world, and Lindbergh was instantly catapulted to fame. Between three and four and a half million people turned out for Lindbergh's parade in New York City, far exceeding the numbers at the parade celebrating the end of the First World War. From July 20 to October 23 of the same year, Lindbergh flew *The Spirit of St. Louis* around the country, visiting all forty-eight states. Lindbergh's flight and his promotion of civil aviation marked a turning point in the commercial aviation industry in America.

From 1927 to 1932, Lindbergh took up the role of an ambassador of good will for America. Ludovic Kennedy, author of a book about Lindbergh, speaks about the unusual charisma that Lindbergh possessed: "Lindbergh had already demonstrated to the world his skill as an airman. Now he was showing another, quite unexpected quality: that when he spoke, people listened; that he had an outstanding natural authority."[18]

Walter S. Ross, author of a biography of Lindbergh, speaks of the effect of these visits: "In each of the countries in which he landed, he demonstrated his friendliness toward the inhabitants and helped reestablish the image of Uncle Sam as a benevolent fellow."[19] In December 1927, the House and the Senate voted unanimously to award Lindbergh the Congressional Medal of Honor, an award previously reserved only for military heroes.

Lindbergh with *The Spirit of St. Louis,* May 31, 1927

## Anne Morrow

In the same month, on a good-will visit to Mexico, Lindbergh met Anne Morrow, daughter of the U.S. Ambassador. Anne Morrow described her meeting with Lindbergh as love at first sight. In her diary she described his reception in Mexico, where the crowd was shouting *Viva Lindbergh:* "Who has moved like that before, not with a speech, not intentionally, not trying to move them by any means—just standing there, just existing."[20]

But there was a price for the fame. "He could no longer walk anywhere freely; he was mobbed wherever he went. . . . If he sent anything to a laundry, it didn't come back; he was always buying new shirts and underwear. If he checked a hat it was somehow 'lost.' If he wrote a bank check it would not be cashed but kept as a souvenir for his autograph."[21]

Charles and Anne Morrow Lindbergh

In 1928, Lindbergh went to work for Pan American Airways and Transcontinental Air Transport (later called TWA) as a technical consultant, surveying new air routes and providing other technical assistance in setting up commercial air operations. In the fall of that same year, Lindbergh was surprised to find himself thinking more and more of Anne Morrow, and he laid plans to meet her again. After two dates, they were engaged to be married. They married on May 27, 1929, in a small private ceremony. To avoid publicity, even the guests were not told the reason for the invitation.

Ross writes of the relationship: "In many ways they were opposite. Her interests were literary; she yearned to be a writer; she had graduated with special honors from Smith College. Lindbergh, the college dropout, was interested in mechanical things that went fast, and in science. Where she was very contemplative he was adventurous. But they shared many traits of character. They were both shy; both were solitaries; both had lively, questing minds. They both loved nature. They had very similar ideas about integrity and service and what one owed to one's country."[22]

In 1930, Lindbergh ordered a plane from Lockheed specially built for him. He named it *Sirius*. He continued his work scouting new routes for commercial air service, and his wife accompanied him as navigator on flights to Asia, Europe, Africa and Latin America.

## The Crime of the Decade

The Lindberghs' son, Charles Augustus Lindbergh Jr., was born on June 22, 1930. Less than two years later, March 1, 1932, he was kidnapped from their home near Hopewell, New Jersey. Because of Lindbergh's worldwide fame, the kidnapping became the most notorious crime of the 1930s. Al Capone even offered a $10,000 reward for the return of the child. (It would be interesting to know if they had any karmic connection from previous lives.) On April 2, a $50,000 ransom was paid, but on May 12, the baby's body was discovered about a mile from the Lindbergh home.

On August 16 of that year, the Lindberghs' second son, Jon, was born, and in 1935, Lindbergh took his family to England to escape the press and the public hysteria about the case. Journalist H. L. Mencken described the trial as "the biggest story since the Resurrection,"[23] and at one point, Lindbergh was receiving 100,000 letters a day.

Some of the gold certificates used to pay the ransom eventually resurfaced and were traced to Richard Hauptmann, who was convicted of the kidnapping and murder and sent to the electric chair on April 3, 1936. However, Ludovic Kennedy argues that Hauptmann was not responsible and that the police investigating the case manufactured evidence that was crucial to Hauptmann's conviction.

Lindbergh testifying at the trial of Richard Hauptmann. Journalist H. L. Mencken described the trial as "the biggest story since the Resurrection."

## The Second World War

In the years of 1939 to 1941, Lindbergh campaigned against American intervention in the European war. He explained his position in this way:

> I felt that I could exercise a constructive influence in America by warning people of the danger of the Soviet Union, and by explaining that the destruction of Hitler, even if it could be accomplished through using American resources, would probably result in enhancing the still greater menace of Stalin. I would argue for an American policy of strength and neutrality.... If [the European nations] prostrated themselves once again in internecine war, then at least one strong Western nation would remain to protect Western civilization.[24]

In his book *Autobiography of Values*, published posthumously, Lindbergh explained that he believed how of the two dictatorships of Hitler and Stalin, Stalin posed the greatest threat. He believed that Hitler would eventually die and the Germans would moderate the excesses of his regime, but that the ruthlessness and terror of the Soviets far exceeded anything the Germans had done up to that time. His greatest hope was that war would be confined to fighting between Hitler and Stalin.

Lindbergh may have underestimated the depth of evil in Hitler, but his assessment of the two regimes at that time is not without foundation. Hitler's antisemitism was already apparent, but Lindbergh's campaign against intervention in the war was years before the Holocaust, while Stalin had already killed 7.5 million Ukrainians through intentional famine in 1932–33 and an estimated 13 to 15 million Russians in the political purges of the late 1930s.[25]

Lindbergh was a powerful spokesman for neutrality, and President Roosevelt offered Lindbergh the post of First Secretary of a new separate Air Force if he would support Roosevelt's position of aid to France and England short of war. However, Lindbergh formed an astute opinion of Roosevelt after a fifteen-minute meeting with him at the White House on April 15, 1939. In his *Autobiography of Values,* Lindbergh wrote:

> He is an accomplished, suave, interesting conversationalist.... I liked him and feel that I could get along well with him. Acquaintanceship would be pleasant and interesting.
>
> But there was something about him I did not trust, something a little too suave, too pleasant, too easy. Still, he is our President, and there is no reason for any antagonism between us in the work that I am now doing....
>
> Roosevelt judges his man quickly and plays him cleverly. He is mostly politician, and I think that we would

> never get along on many fundamentals. But there are things about him I like, and why worry about the others unless and until they necessitate consideration? It is better to work together as long as we can: yet somehow I have a feeling that it may not be for long.[26]

Roosevelt's problem was that he faced re-election in 1940. He was in favor of intervention in the war, and in 1939 the polls showed seventy percent of Americans wanted to stay completely neutral. Lindbergh became the most effective spokesman for America First, the major organization opposing intervention in the war. Roosevelt saw that the combination of Lindbergh's prestige and the breadth of popular support for the isolationist position could have been insurmountable barriers to his re-election.

Roosevelt's response to this threat was to go on the offensive, ordering the IRS to "get Lindbergh." When that didn't work, Roosevelt tried to portray Lindbergh as pro-Nazi. Ross comments: "Lindbergh was a strong and dangerous political antagonist, never a potential traitor. But Roosevelt had to get rid of him at any cost."[27]

On December 11, 1941, following the Japanese attack on Pearl Harbor, America First issued a statement: "Our principles were right. Had they been followed, war could have been avoided. No good purpose can now be served by considering what might have been.... We are at war... the primary objective is... victory."[28]

Lindbergh was never a pacifist. He believed that military strength was essential to America's security, and on December 30, 1941, he volunteered to re-enlist in the Air Corps. Roosevelt would not let go of his vendetta against Lindbergh and refused to allow him to enlist. Lindbergh applied to work for United Aircraft and Curtiss-Wright, but both companies were told that employing Lindbergh would be frowned upon by Washington.

Lindbergh with Thomas Edison (center) and Henry Ford (right). Lindbergh and Ford were lifelong friends—perhaps they had known each other on Atlantis, when Ford was working on developments to the *vailx* that allowed transoceanic aerial travel.

Without asking permission from the government, Henry Ford asked Lindbergh to work at his B-24 assembly plant. Lindbergh's lifelong friendship with Ford had begun some years earlier, when Lindbergh took Ford for his first and only airplane ride, in *The Spirit of St. Louis.* Ford was also affiliated with America First. Both Lindbergh and Ford believed in reincarnation.

In 1944, Lindbergh got United Aircraft to appoint him as a technical representative to evaluate aircraft performance under combat conditions. The only way to do this was to fly the planes in combat situations, and in six months in the Pacific Lindbergh flew a full complement of fifty combat missions as a civilian, the same number as personnel in the armed services. Lindbergh also developed innovations in operating procedures that shortened the war by several months and saved thousands of American lives.

## After the War

In 1946, after the end of the war, Lindbergh went to Germany to survey German aviation and rocketry for the U.S. Government. He said of this experience, "In Germany, I learned that if his civilization is to continue, modern man must direct the material power of his science by the spiritual truths of his God."[29]

He took up again his technical consultancy with Pan Am. He also bought a house in a secluded part of Connecticut in order to provide his children with the sort of childhood that Lindbergh himself had not had.

In 1954, Lindbergh won the Pulitzer Prize for his book *The Spirit of St. Louis,* which was made into a movie starring James Stewart in 1957. In the same year he was nominated by Eisenhower for a commission as Brigadier General in the U.S. Air Force Reserve—righting some of the wrong done to him by Roosevelt.

From 1964 to 1974, the last ten years of his life, Lindbergh increasingly devoted his energies to conservation projects. In his later years, he also became interested in religion and spirituality. As a young man he was enthralled with science, but later in life he said, "To live, man needs both science and religion."[30] He died on Maui on August 26, 1974, at the age of 72.

## Lindbergh's Spiritual Life

Ross comments that "Lindbergh himself has explored the occult, though with a practical purpose in mind. He once studied Yoga to learn how bodily processes could be controlled. He had the idea that if people could learn to stop their heartbeat, it might be useful in surgery. He did learn how to stop his own pulse, or, at least, to make it imperceptible."[31]

In his autobiography, Lindbergh tells of a spiritual experience he had during the twenty-second hour of his transatlantic flight in the *Spirit of St. Louis.* Due to nervousness about the upcoming flight, he had not slept the evening before his departure, and he was consequently struggling to stay awake while piloting the plane.

> I had been without sleep for nearly two days and two nights. My conscious mind had lost control of its body. My movements were made by instinct, not by will.

Then he became aware of what he called "phantoms" grouped in the fuselage behind him.

> Gradually, the apparent difference between self and phantoms faded and I, too, existed independently of time and matter. I felt myself departing from my body as I imagine a spirit would depart—emanating into the cockpit, extending through the fuselage as though no frame or fabric walls were there, angling upward, outward, until I re-formed in an awareness far distant from the human form I left in a fast-flying transatlantic plane. But I remained connected to my body through a long-extended strand, a strand related to the form of man, a strand so tenuous that it could have been severed by a breath, an ethereal breath unrelated to the propeller's wash.
>
> Then I re-formed slowly as a man again, returning from spatial distances to my plane and body, condensing and collapsing into earthly qualities.[32]

The Indian saint Paramahansa Yogananda said that Lindbergh had been embodied not only as Abraham Lincoln but also in an earlier time as an Indian yogi. While this last life was one of intense action in the world, his mystical bent came to the fore in his later years—and was perhaps a strength supporting him throughout his life.

## The Thread of Karma

The death of the firstborn son is a theme that carried through Lindbergh's three lives in very public and dramatic ways. The pharaoh of Egypt lost his firstborn in the tenth plague; Lincoln was crushed when he lost his son Willie to typhoid in 1862; and Lindbergh's first son was kidnapped and murdered. The same soul returned as Lindbergh's son in each embodiment, and according to Mark Prophet, three times was the requirement of the Law for the full working out of this particular karma.[33]

Who knows how far back the karma went? No mention is made by either Mark or Elizabeth Prophet of lifetimes of Lindbergh on Atlantis or Lemuria, but like the other lifestreams in this study, Lindbergh must have been there. The karmic roots of the life of the pharaoh no doubt lie in that ancient past. Perhaps his associations with Henry Ford and FDR that were so important in this life had also their origins in that era.

Many hoped that Lindbergh would run for president in the election of 1940, and this was probably one reason for Roosevelt's vendetta against him—he saw him as a political rival. It is likely Lindbergh would have won. Not only his evident charisma in this life, but also the soul recognition of the American people of Lincoln come again would have been a powerful impetus towards that victory. However, he did not enter the race, and people speculate as to the reasons for this. Perhaps the soul memory of a previous life led him not to walk that path again. Perhaps having faced the power elite of his day as Lincoln, it was simply not his calling in his next life.

Ann Rutledge was Lincoln's twin flame, and their brief connection was a key to inspiring Lincoln for his mission in that life. They were united again when she reembodied as Anne Morrow, and perhaps the fact that this time they could be together for many years was a sign that karma that had separated them had been balanced.[34]

## An American Hero

Lindbergh had enormous talent and heroism, but more than this it is the character of the man that stands out—his willingness to speak his mind, a presence that moved people, a great desire for public service, and of course a level of popular adulation almost unparalleled in the twentieth century. The fact that he was unmoved by this says something of the character of the man—and perhaps also of his becoming accustomed to the challenges of a very public life in previous embodiments.

Abraham Lincoln once said:

> If I were to try to read, much less answer, all the attacks made on me, this shop might as well be closed for any other business. I do the very best I know how—the very best I can; and I mean to keep doing so until the end. If the end brings me out all right, what is said against me won't amount to anything. If the end brings me out wrong, ten thousand angels swearing I was right would make no difference.[35]

Along with Lincoln, Lindbergh is considered by many to be an American hero. Yet Lindbergh also seems to invoke extreme judgments—while even some former enemies have called him a saint, others continue to insist that he was a Nazi.

So what happens to a soul who made grave karma a long time ago, who strove to balance that karma and made great progress over thousands of years—not a perfect man, but one who is striving and perhaps not quite ready to make his ascension?

Charles Lindbergh has re-embodied with the opportunity to balance the accounts that remain to be settled in his life.

George Herman "Babe" Ruth, Jr. (1895–1948)

CHAPTER 9

# Babe Ruth

*By the Editors*

The eighth of the nine individuals studied in Elizabeth Clare Prophet's lecture was to have been Babe Ruth, the most famous American baseball player of all time. We are including here a brief account of his life, which shows both positive and negative momentums that must surely have been carried over from previous lives. Mark and Elizabeth Prophet have not spoken of Babe Ruth or his past lives, so we leave it to the reader to ponder the lessons of this life.

---

George Herman Ruth, Jr., was born in his grandparents' house near the waterfront section of Baltimore on February 6, 1895. His parents were German-American. His father was a bartender in a combination saloon and grocery store. His mother had poor health and tried to help her husband as much as she could in the saloon. His parents had seven more children, six of whom died in infancy—only Mary Margaret and George survived to adulthood.

Babe Ruth (right) at age 7, soon after he was admitted to St. Mary's

Lawrence Ritter, author of a biography of Ruth, describes his childhood: "The youngster never had a real childhood in the usual sense of the word. His earliest memories were of street fights, stealing from shopkeepers, throwing rocks at deliverymen, and fleeing from cops through narrow cobblestoned alleys. He rarely went to school and for all practical purposes survived on the streets without direction or supervision."[1]

It seems that his parents didn't know what to do with George, Jr., and at the age of 7 they sent him to St. Mary's Industrial School, a reformatory and orphanage in Baltimore, where he spent most of the next twelve years. His parents rarely visited, and his mother died when he was 12.

While students at St. Mary's did receive some education, the primary emphasis was on work, and Ruth learned the trade of a shirtmaker. Discipline was strict, reinforced by frequent corporal punishment. Brother Matthias Boutlier was the school's disciplinarian—not someone you would expect to be popular in a place like St. Mary's, but the boys respected his strength and fairness.

Ruth would later tell writer Bob Considine that Brother Matthias was "the greatest man I've ever known.... He was the father I needed. He taught me to read and write—and he taught me the difference between right and wrong."[2]

Robert Creamer, author of another biography, describes the unlikely bond that developed between Ruth and Brother Matthias:

> Ruth revered Brother Matthias, . . . which is remarkable, considering that Matthias was in charge of making boys behave and that Ruth was one of the great natural misbehavers of all time. . . .
>
> George Ruth caught Brother Matthias' attention early, and the calm, considerate attention the big man gave the young hellraiser from the waterfront struck a spark of response in the boy's soul. The spark did not seem to do much in the way of making Ruth into a polished soft-spoken gentleman, but it may have pulled some of the sharper claws and blunted a few of the more savage teeth in the gross man whom I have heard at least a half-dozen of his baseball contemporaries describe with admiring awe and wonder as "an animal."[3]

## Baseball

Most of the boys at St. Mary's played baseball, and Brother Matthias, a capable player himself, helped the boy develop his natural talent. George played all positions in his time at St. Mary's, but came to prominence as the best pitcher at the school. In early 1914, he was signed to a professional baseball contract by Jack Dunn, owner and manager of a minor-league team, the Baltimore Orioles. There was one problem that had to be overcome: Ruth was not able to leave St. Mary's until he was 21 except to return to the care of his parents. Dunn found an ingenious solution by becoming Ruth's legal guardian.

Ruth explains how he got his nickname: "On the first day of spring training, Dunn practically led me by the hand from the dressing room to the pitcher's box. I was as proud of my Orioles' uniform as I had been of my first long pants. Maybe I showed that pride in my face and the way I walked. 'Look at Dunnie and his new babe,' yelled one of the older players."[4] The name stayed with him for the rest of his life.

The Orioles were very successful with Ruth as their star pitcher, but the team was having financial problems, and on July 4, 1914, Dunn sold Ruth's contract to the Boston Red Sox for a reported $25,000. Ruth had arrived in the major leagues at the age of 19.

Ruth arrived in Boston on July 11. He used to tell the story of being served breakfast that morning by a 16-year-old waitress, Helen Woodford. They married on October 14.

Ruth achieved great success as a pitcher for the Red Sox, winning a World Series for them in 1916 and again in 1918. In the second match he pitched 29 consecutive scoreless innings, a record that was not broken until 1961. He was possibly the best left-handed pitcher in baseball at that time, but what he really wanted to do was hit baseballs.

In 1919, he had his chance. By late June it was clear that the Red Sox were out of contention for the series title, and their manager, Ed Barrow, was willing to allow his star pitcher to concentrate on his hitting. Ruth began an unprecedented string of hitting home runs. On June 29, he broke the American League single-season record of 16, which had been set in 1902. On September 8, he reached the major-league mark of 24, and he finished the season with a record 29 home runs. He became a national sensation, and crowds turned out to see his games in record numbers.

There is some mystery as to why Red Sox owner, Harry Frazee, decided to sell Ruth to the New York Yankees after this record-breaking season. There is speculation that he needed the money to pay for a theatrical venture. The Yankees paid $100,000 for Ruth, the largest sum ever for a baseball player up to that time.

Ruth continued slugging home runs for the Yankees. The team finished third in the series, but fans came out in record numbers to see the spectacle of Babe Ruth at the plate. The Yankees had 1.2 million fans at their home games, the first ever seven-figure attendance. The rest of the league sold 600,000 more tickets than the previous season, many of them to people who came to see Babe Ruth hit baseballs out of the park. He led the league with 54 home runs that season.

Late in the 1920 season, it was discovered that eight members of the Chicago White Sox had been bribed by gamblers to give the 1919 World Series to the Cincinnati Reds. Fans were enormously disillusioned. Creamer comments:

> That professional baseball survived, and even prospered, is due in good measure to Babe Ruth. His exploits overshadowed the shameful events of 1919 and soon eclipsed them. His tape-measure homers[5] and magnetic personality so captured the imagination of the public that baseball soared in popularity and attendance reached unprecedented heights despite the scandal.[6]

## A Wild Life off the Field

Ruth was larger-than-life off the field as well as on. He had enormous appetites for food and drink and a reputation for womanizing. Biographer Leigh Montville describes life with Babe Ruth from the perspective of Waite Hoyt, a 21-year-old teammate who became a close friend:

> The outrageous life fascinated Hoyt, the don't-give-a-[damn] freedom of it, the nonstop, pell-mell charge into excess. How did a man drink so much and never get drunk? . . . The puzzle of Babe Ruth never was dull, no matter how many times Hoyt picked up the pieces and stared at them.
>
> After games he would follow the crowd to the Babe's

> suite. No matter what the town, the beer would be iced and the bottles would fill the bathtub.[7]

Early in 1922, the New York Yankees signed Ruth to a five-year contract at an unprecedented $50,000 per year. Colonel Til Huston, co-owner of the team, told Ruth:

> We are tying up a lot of money in you, Babe, far more than any player ever has received, and we feel you should give us something in return, not only hitting home runs, but in your conduct. We know you've often been drinking and whoring all hours of the night, and paying no attention to training rules. As we are giving you a quarter of a million for the next five years, we want you to act with more responsibility. You can drink beer and enjoy cards *and* be in your room by eleven o'clock, the same as the other players. It still gives you a lot of time to have a good time.

Ruth replied:

> Colonel, I'll promise to go easier on drinking, and get to bed earlier. But, not for you, fifty thousand dollars, or two hundred fifty thousand dollars will I give up women. They're too much fun.[8]

Many years later, sportswriter Fred Lieb commented on Ruth's womanizing: "A believer in reincarnation, I always have felt that Ruth was a reincarnated African king or an Arabic emir with a stable of wives and concubines."[9]

Ruth and his wife, Helen, had adopted an infant daughter, Dorothy, in 1921, and the child brought them much happiness. But the wild lifestyle took its toll on their marriage. The couple separated around 1925, reportedly because of his repeated infidelities. Divorce negotiations were begun, but fell apart. Helen died in a fire in January 1929, and Ruth married Claire Hodgson, a pretty young widow from Georgia, three months later.

Babe Ruth, Helen and their daughter, Dorothy, 1925

## The House That Ruth Built

Meanwhile, Babe Ruth continued to break records on the baseball field. The Yankees built a new stadium for the 1923 season, and he scored the first home run in the stadium that soon came to be known as "The House That Ruth Built." The venue was built with their star player in mind—the right-field fence was closer to the plate than their previous stadium, making it easier for a left-hander like Ruth to hit home runs.

The 1927 Yankees team is considered to have been one of the greatest line-ups ever to take the field. They so dominated the season that there was little suspense in the race for the pennant. The nation's attention turned instead to Ruth's pursuit of his own home-run season record. He broke it with his career high of 60 on September 30. "Sixty! Let's see some son of a bitch try to top that one,"[10] Ruth said, in his typical style, after the game.

Seattle, 1924

For the 1928 season, Ruth signed a new contract for an astronomical $80,000 per year. When someone asked him in 1930 whether he thought he should make so much, when the President, Herbert Hoover, made $75,000, Ruth is said to have answered: "Why not? I had a better year than he did."[11] (The Great Depression had begun the previous year.)

If there is one episode that exemplifies the magic of Babe Ruth at bat, it is perhaps the legendary hit in the fifth inning of game 3 of the 1932 World Series at Wrigley Field in Chicago. The score was tied at 4–4, and the Babe was at bat. He was being mercilessly heckled by the Chicago Cubs' players on the bench, and the crowd was jeering and throwing fruit. After one strike, Ruth raised his arm and pointed towards center field. Another strike. He raised his arm and pointed to center field again. His third attempt was a huge hit that landed in the stands beyond the deepest part of center field.

1933

## Retirement

Ruth left the Yankees in 1934 after leading them to seven pennants. His career as a player was nearly over, but he played twenty-nine games with the Boston Braves in 1935 before retiring from active competition. He lobbied heavily for a job as a manager, but no one would hire him. Some thought it was because of his reckless lifestyle off the field. Yankees general manager Ed Barrow summed it up: "How can he manage other men when he can't even manage himself?"[12] His daughter said in later years it was because he would have hired black players for his team—at a time when the sport was strictly (though unofficially) segregated.[13]

Ruth played a lot of golf and a few exhibition baseball games, continuing to draw crowds wherever he went. He made many personal appearances to support the war effort during the 1940s, and his last appearance as a player was at Yankee Stadium in 1943 for the Army-Navy Relief Fund. He made one last hit that left the field. It curved foul, but he ran the bases anyway.

Doctors urged him to take better care of his health, and he

limited his drinking somewhat. In 1946, he began to experience severe pain over his left eye and difficulty swallowing, and in November tests revealed throat cancer. (He had been smoking and chewing tobacco since the age of 7 and often smoked a dozen cigars a day when he was older.) An experimental chemotherapy treatment gave hope for a while, but the disease soon resumed its course.

On June 13, 1948, the Yankees celebrated the twenty-fifth anniversary of Yankee Stadium, the field that had been built for him. Ruth made a final appearance, putting on his uniform for the last time.

Thousands of New Yorkers kept a vigil outside Memorial Hospital in his last days. He died in his sleep on August 16, 1948, at the age of 53. His casket was taken to Yankee Stadium, where 77,000 people filed past to pay tribute. His funeral Mass was held in New York's Saint Patrick's Cathedral. The cathedral was full, with an estimated 75,000 people outside.

There were star players in baseball before, but none had enthralled the public in the way Babe Ruth did. The record for career home runs before Ruth was 138. Ruth had hit 714 by the time he retired. He had risen from the mean streets of Baltimore's waterfront and an upbringing in a reform school to become the most famous person in America.

## Transcending Circumstance

Ruth transcended his sport to become a national hero. He was uncouth, brash and unbeatable, in some ways epitomizing the spirit of a new nation taking its place on the world scene. But there was also another side to his character.

In 1947, he established the Babe Ruth Foundation to aid underprivileged youth, and he often made headlines visiting sick children in hospital. Sportswriter Tom Meany once said, "You have to understand that his affection for children was sincere.

Crowds at Yankee Stadium waiting to pay their respects

The Babe, for all of his lusty living, for all of his bluff and often crude ways, had ever a soft spot in his heart for kids."[14]

Perhaps this is one lesson from the life of Babe Ruth. He never forgot the 7-year-old boy who was abandoned by his parents and sent to an orphanage. He could have become angry at them—or at God—for the seeming injustice of it all. Looking at his life as a child, a petty criminal running wild on the streets, it would not have been at all surprising to see him follow a similar course to Al Capone.

Why did Babe Ruth make such a different choice when faced with what seems to have been an even more difficult karmic circumstance?

Perhaps it was that he had a better mentor in Brother Matthias than Capone had in Johnny Torrio. Perhaps the answer to the puzzle would be revealed in the reading of his previous lives. Or perhaps what we see is simply the outplaying of the inner essence of the soul—proof of the supremacy of free will.

Elizabeth Clare Prophet (1939–2009)

CHAPTER 10

# Elizabeth Clare Prophet

The last lifestream that El Morya assigned in this series is my own. I am not bringing you all of my lifetimes but key lifetimes and especially those that have shaped me, molded me, and brought me to where I am today.

First of all, I remember leaving the Great Central Sun. I remember going before Alpha and Omega, our Father-Mother God in the great throne room, bowing before them, and asking their leave to go and descend into the lower octaves where the rebel angels, those who had rebelled against God and his Christ, were moving against the children of Light. I specifically asked permission to go and find them and woo them back to God. I received the blessing of beloved Alpha and Omega to do this.

The teaching that they gave me before I departed was that I would go forth and for many long centuries I would be mother to them and teacher to them. But when their time of opportunity for repentance would have concluded, then I would be in the position of calling forth their judgment.

They said to me that the mission did not have a great chance of success, but they would support me in my efforts. They said that these reprobate ones would woo me and flatter me and support me so long as I was to them mother and teacher, but that when the time of their judgment would come—and they, Alpha and Omega, would send me the message that the judgment hour had come—they would rise up against me and make war against me.

I remember clearly the record of descending down what I can only describe as a chute of light like a large tunnel. I went down and down and down until I came to the octaves of earth to which I was sent. This was in a timeless epoch, and I cannot give you a date for it.

Sometime after this, I did journey to earth with Sanat Kumara as part of the band of those who would come and help to establish the rekindling of the threefold flame in those in whom it had gone out.

---

**LIFE NUMBER 1:** Place: Atlantis
Sex: Female

The first life we consider is Atlantis. I was a High Priestess of the Divine Mother on Atlantis. And I have a recollection of celebrating the rite of the regeneration of spring.

I will give life number 2 at the conclusion of the others.

---

**LIFE NUMBER 3:** Place: Egypt
Date: c. 1370 to c. 1330 BC
Sex: Female

I was embodied as Nefertiti, the wife of the Egyptian Pharaoh Ikhnaton, originally known as Amenhotep IV. In the fifth year of his reign, around 1348 BC, Ikhnaton converted to the worship of Aton, the one God. Aton is often depicted as a sun disc with rays stretching forth ending in hands.

Ikhnaton established a new capital city at Amarna and started a revolution in art as well as religion. He and his queen officiated as high priest and priestess. They had six daughters. Paintings of the King and Queen displayed them in many intimate and touching domestic scenes that revealed the depth of their love and the closeness of their family life.

Ikhnaton issued an ultimatum that all of the old gods, the false gods, must go. He launched a religious war. Ikhnaton ordered all idols of Amon to be destroyed. A rising tide of hatred fed by the priests of Amon threatened to engulf the royal family. Around the fourteenth year of Ikhnaton's reign, Nefertiti disappeared from public view. She was replaced by Smenkhare, the husband of their eldest daughter. Some believe she was banished to the northern part of the city; others that she withdrew voluntarily.

In the seventeenth year of Ikhnaton's reign, he, his wife, Smenkhare and the eldest daughter disappeared. Scholars have guessed that they were murdered. By whom and when and how is unknown. El Morya has showed me that it was the chief military man, General Horemheb, who led a revolt against Ikhnaton and Nefertiti and stabbed them to death. I remember the scene very clearly of running down the halls of a great palace being pursued by the men of Horemheb. After the death of Ikhnaton and Nefertiti, the country reverted to the worship of the old gods of Egypt.

At about the age of four in this life, when I was playing in the sand in my play yard in Red Bank, New Jersey, I was suddenly transported and I was playing in the sand on the banks of the Nile River in Egypt. I was a child, with my mother tending me, and I had a sense that my mother was royal.

This could well have been harking back thirty-three centuries to the time of Nefertiti and Ikhnaton, and I believe that it was, because this was the century marked by God for Mark Prophet and I to come together again and to once more restore the true worship of the one God and to reveal the knowledge and understanding of the I AM THAT I AM.

Ikhnaton, Nefertiti and three of their daughters under the rays of Aton

It is said that Moses took his monotheism from the teachings of Ikhnaton of the one God.[1] And, of course, Incal was the great God of Atlantis, the one God represented in the sun, and Ikhnaton brought that teaching and he gave the image of the sun with rays going forth ending in hands, meaning that we are the hand of God in action.

I think it's very important that I had that experience, and I would not have had it without the overshadowing presence of beloved El Morya. It was necessary that I make the tie to this key embodiment in which I made karma that I had to balance in this life, among other karmas. That memory also brought me back to the point of the mission to establish a new religion based on the old order of the traditions of the world's major religions.

**LIFE NUMBER 4:** Place: Palestine
Date: First century AD
Sex: Female

I lived in Palestine in the first century AD as Jesus' disciple Martha of Bethany. I lived at Bethany with my brother Lazarus and sister Mary. We were close friends of Jesus Christ. He stayed in our home whenever he came to Jerusalem. Those of you who have toured the Holy Land know that Bethany is just a short distance outside of Jerusalem.

Martha was the head of the household and appears to have been the eldest in the family. She cooked for Jesus and looked after his physical needs when he would visit. Harriet Beecher Stowe wrote, in her book called *Women in Sacred History*: "Martha was one of those natural leaders whom everybody instinctively thinks of as the head of any house they may happen to belong to."[2] It's very interesting that my childhood playmate in this life was the re-embodiment of Harriet Beecher Stowe. She had already written about Martha in that life and then we spent our earliest childhood together. From age 2 to 9 we were inseparable.

Martha is known for her confession of faith in Jesus Christ. It happened after her brother Lazarus had died and Jesus came to Bethany. Martha and Mary had sent word to Jesus when Lazarus became ill, but he did not go to Bethany immediately. By the time he arrived, Lazarus had already been in the grave for four days. We read in John, chapter 11:

> Then Martha, as soon as she heard that Jesus was coming, went and met him: but Mary sat still in the house. Then said Martha unto Jesus, "Lord, if thou hadst been here, my brother had not died. But I know, that even now, whatsoever thou wilt ask of God, he will give it thee."

> Jesus saith unto her: "Thy brother shall rise again." Martha saith unto him, "I know that he shall rise again in the resurrection at the last day." Jesus said unto her, "I am the resurrection, and the life: he that believeth in me, though he were dead, yet shall he live: And whosoever liveth and believeth in me shall never die. Believest thou this?"
>
> She saith unto him, "Yea, Lord: I believe that thou art the Christ, the Son of God, which should come into the world."

Strong traditions indicate that following the crucifixion of Jesus, Martha went to France to propagate his teachings. Her relics are in the church dedicated to her in Tarascon, France.

Mary, the sister of Martha, reembodied as Mary Baker Eddy and brought forth the teachings of Jesus Christ, Mother Mary and the apostle Paul in her Christian Science textbook, *Science and Health with Key to the Scriptures,* and her other writings. What she wrote down, what she received from God, sponsored by Jesus and Paul and Mother Mary, was not the whole truth of divine science. She spoke about her glimpse of divine science and that the full realization and the full statement of that divine science was yet to come. She distinguished between Christian Science, the religion and the church she founded, and divine science as a universal science.[3]

When I was searching for a church between the ages of 7 and 9, I chose the Christian Science church because, as I told my parents, it was the church that taught me the most about God and Jesus. I am certain that I was drawn to it because it was the highest truth available to me in my town. I have a very great love for Mary Baker Eddy and for Mary, the sister of Martha and Lazarus—a profound devotion to her heart. She is now an ascended lady master.

**LIFE NUMBER 5:** Place: France
Date: 474 to 545 AD
Sex: Female

Clotilde, daughter of Chilperic, King of the Burgundians of Lyon, was a devout Christian with a very strong belief in God. According to the legends, her father and mother were killed by Chilperic's brother Gondebad, who seized the throne of Burgundy and held the young princess as a prisoner for 15 years.

Clovis, King of the Franks, was a pagan at the time. The story goes that he had heard of the beauty of Clotilde and sent out his messenger to see if this was true. This messenger arrived at the castle of Gondebad, and she welcomed him in the Christian tradition of washing his feet. He considered this a sign of humility, took note of her beauty, and arranged for the marriage. Gondebad, fearing the power of the Franks and hoping to benefit from an alliance with their king, initially agreed.

Clotilde feared that her uncle would soon change his mind, so she arranged to leave as soon as she could be taken to Clovis. And in her anger against what her uncle had done to her and her family, as she was leaving, she set fire to peasant huts of straw that were the homes of the servants of the king.

This is a very interesting story because very early in my training as a messenger, just a few days before a conference we were having in Washington, D.C., I was heating some fat at high temperature on the stove and pouring the fat from the frying pan into a cup. I poured it over my hand and sustained quite a serious burn. I put it in cold water and wrapped it and so forth. Mark told me that this was a token of karma that I had incurred because I set fire to those peasants' huts. No one died but their homes were destroyed.

A little leaven leavens the whole lump. Sometimes when we have been in the service of God for centuries and performed good deeds, God gives us just a small percentage so that that will balance that karma and so that we can learn the lesson of life. This is an example of the mercy of God. I didn't have to have my house burned down in order to pay that karmic debt.

El Morya said I could not enter that conference and take the lecture platform and stand before the people with that karma on my soul. And therefore it had to be cleared by my experiencing that burning. My hand had a scar for many years, and I was grateful because it could remind me of the mercy of God.

In this embodiment as Clotilde, I undertook to convert Clovis to the Christian religion. In the year 496, in the midst of a battle against the Alemanni, Clovis vowed to convert to Christianity if Clotilde's God would grant him victory. Clovis won the battle and was baptized. Clotilde was thus instrumental in the conversion of the Frankish people to the Christian faith. After Clovis' death, she spent her life in prayer and service to her people.

---

**LIFE NUMBER 6:** Place: Denmark
Date: c. 890 AD
Sex: Female

I was born into a family of fishermen in Denmark. When I grew up, a young fisherman was attracted to me. I was not much interested in him. He went out on a long fishing trip with his father. I can see the ships coming in. I can see the women and children going to greet these ships and receive their husbands, their fathers, their sons back from the long trip.

I am seeing them coming off the boat and coming up the path. I see this one coming toward my house. And I am in my kitchen and I am preparing a meal and I have a carving knife in my hand. I am cutting up vegetables. He came into my house as I was preparing this meal, and he came at me and he desired me. I rebuffed him and therefore he raped me. I was outraged. The knife was in my hand, and in my rage against this offense, I killed him. This was certainly one of the most tragic events in my history.

I lived this life out and I went before the Lords of Karma. And I can remember that scene very clearly also. I knelt before them and I was sobbing. I said to them, "I will do anything to balance this karma. I will serve this person as long as you will have me serve him. Let me give him back the life that I took from him." And so the Lords of Karma assigned me to a number of embodiments where I could serve him.

The amazing teaching in this matter is that the crime of murder is not justified by the crime of rape. We must all remember this when we feel the anger within our souls rise up at the violation of our bodies.

---

**LIFE NUMBER 7:** Place: Japan
Date: c. 900 AD
Sex: Female

This next life was one of the lifetimes in which the Lords of Karma graciously gave me the opportunity to balance this karma. It was Japan. I was born poor, and I was forced to marry a man I did not love. He became a cripple. We lived in abject poverty, eating next to nothing.

This man was the soul I had killed in Denmark. And I had to serve him to balance the karma of murder and also to learn the lesson that this body is the Body of God, that God will do what he wills with this body and I cannot harm another except if the crime is the equivalent. In other words, if someone is about to kill me, I may kill in self-defense if I choose to. But rape does not justify murder.

---

**LIFE NUMBER 8:** Place: Japan
Date: c. 980 AD
Sex: Female

I returned to Japan just eighty years later. I was very intent on balancing this karma, and the Lords of Karma gave me the opportunity. I was married to the same man again. This time, strangely enough, he was a taxidermist and supported us. I served him as his wife. By the end of that life, the karma of the murder was still not paid off, and I had to finish paying it off in this current life. It is amazing that in a moment of rashness we can commit a crime that takes us three embodiments to pay off.

The amazing teaching that I received in this life regarding this situation is that this karma had to be balanced before I could be called to be a messenger for the ascended masters.

I went to Boston. I served in a Christian Science church. And I saw this young man, about five years older than me. He was a leader in the youth fellowship. He was a law student. He was part Norwegian and part Swedish. I would see him walking around, and the first time I saw him, a block away, I recognized him. It was simply a recognition.

At the same time that I noticed him and recognized him, he recognized me. And it was during this period in my life that I was looking for Saint Germain. When I was leaving home to go to college at the age of 18, I had recognized Saint Germain's picture and he had quickened my heart. I determined I would find him and I would serve him the rest of my life, and I spent the next five years looking for him.

I thought to myself, "I am not finding Saint Germain because I am not ready. Why am I not ready? What am I not doing? What should I be doing?" I thought and thought about it, and I decided the most important thing I must do to find Saint Germain was to be obedient to the voice of God within me. I wrote all over my college books on the paper covers that I made for them, "Obey immediately." I was constantly reminding myself to turn back to the inner voice and to follow the direction of that inner voice.

When I recognized this individual, the inner voice said to me, "You must serve him."

I said, "How shall I serve him?"

"You can help him in his work. You can help him with the youth group."

So I did that. I got to know him. When he was sick, the inner voice said, "Go and take care of him." So I went and I took care of him when he was sick. I kept on receiving these directions of things I should be doing for this person. And I thought, "Well, this is what I will do."

The day came that he asked me to marry him. And I said, "Well, you see, I am looking for Saint Germain. And when I find Saint Germain, I am going to serve him for the rest of my life."

It was kind of meaningless to him. He said, "That's fine," you know. "You can serve him for the rest of your life."

So I said, "Well, on that condition I will marry you."

We were married in a small wedding in New Jersey. And when I came down the aisle at the end of the ceremony, I looked up because I heard the voice of God speaking to me very clearly, "It is but for a little while." I was stunned by this statement because I had married for keeps and I believed in my marriage vows.

We were both going to school in Boston. I quit school to support him so that he could be in school. I kept house, cooked his meals and so forth. I set aside and sacrificed my education so that he could make it. About ten months later, I had found a little group of students of the ascended masters' teachings and they told me that the messenger Mark Prophet was coming from Washington to give a lecture and a dictation. That was April 1961.

I told my husband that I was going to hear a lecture and a dictation and that I had found my contact with Saint Germain. He looked at me and he said, "You'll have to choose between me and Saint Germain."

I said to him, "I already made my choice a long, long time ago."

I went off to hear this lecture and dictation, and the rest is history. But there is more to this story. I was very burdened and could not understand how I had married this person to be only married ten months. How did I make this mistake and why did

I do it? And so I begged Mark to tell me when I went to Washington for the July conference in 1961.

Finally, Mark relented, and he told me of this record of that life in Denmark and of the succeeding embodiments and that the karma had not been balanced until this life. The message from El Morya was that if I had not married this individual and served him, it would have taken me nine years of general service to life to balance that karma.

This lesson tells us it is much easier to balance karma with an individual directly, if at all possible. And if it is indirect, it takes longer. But by the same token, when we are giving the violet flame and serving, we may be balancing karma with thousands of people at the same time.

Had I not obeyed this inner voice and married this individual, I would have postponed my meeting of Saint Germain for nine years. From the time I met Mark Prophet, it was only twelve years till he took his leave from this octave. If I had found him nine years later, which I might not have, I would have only had three years with him. So by being obedient to the inner voice and serving this individual, I finished the balancing of that karma.

I went back home to Boston from that July conference, back to my apartment. There was my husband. And I was in the kitchen one night and I was preparing a meal and I was cutting vegetables with a large knife. He was out in the hallway of our very small apartment, and he started an argument with me. He was yelling at me from the hallway and I was in the kitchen. I forget what the argument was about—nothing is ever significant about arguments. I think that he was just annoyed that I had made the choice for Saint Germain and that it was final.

Knife in hand, I walked out into the hallway, and I started allowing myself to engage in this argument. Then I looked at the knife and I looked at him—I dropped the knife and walked back into the kitchen and kept on with the meal.

I was so very grateful to have had that teaching and to understand that I had come full circle. I was standing at that point in Denmark with that knife in my hand. And by letting go of that knife, this was the end. I had fulfilled that karma and the relationship ended.

El Morya appeared to me in Boston and told me to go to Washington to be trained as a messenger. And I divorced this person. I am sure it was for the better. I haven't been in contact with him since. But I am sure he's had much greater happiness than to be married to me serving Saint Germain when he was a very dedicated Christian Scientist. It was the best that could have happened. And I am profoundly grateful to the Lords of Karma for this guidance.

The moral of the story, of course, is not to take life in the first place, because he who takes life with a sword shall also be killed by the sword. Make your pact with God, listen to his voice in your heart and obey immediately, because you'll never know what turn in the road you will miss if you are not obedient.

Do not be afraid to serve anyone, to sacrifice on anyone's behalf, to surrender yourself because someone needs you in some capacity. Do not be afraid to give of yourself, for you never know when that gift that you give is the paying of the last farthing that will liberate you for the next plane and a higher life.

---

**LIFE NUMBER 9:** Place: Paris
Date: 1110 to 1155
Sex: Female

I was again born into a poor family. I was a washerwoman. I had many children. I think my husband had left somewhere along the way. He doesn't figure much in this life. And I wasted my life. I took care of nine children, took care of their upbringing, but spent altogether too much time chattering over the back fence with neighbors, gossiping and talking. And so my life was lived out as a washerwoman.

It came time for my soul's passing, and I was on my deathbed. A traveling priest came to give me my last rites. I looked into the eyes of this priest and I recognized his eyes—the eyes of my twin flame. One look into his eyes and I saw the vision of our destiny. And I saw how I wasted that life. And so in my last breath I cried out, "Une autre opportunité!"—another opportunity.

He gave me the last rites and moved on. He was just a very plain priest, a humble priest passing by, certainly not by chance. This is one of those brief encounters with your twin flame that ties you together and prepares for a future coming again.

---

**LIFE NUMBER 10:** Place: Assisi, Italy
Date: 1194 to 1253
Sex: Female

This is the life of Clare, devotee of Francis. She was born Chiara Scifi on July 16, 1194, at Assisi, the eldest of five children. Her parents were of noble descent. They lived in a palace in Assisi. Her mother was notably pious. While she was in prayer just before Clare was born, she heard a voice saying to her: "Fear not, Ortolana; thou shalt safely bring forth a light which shall enlighten the whole world clearly."[4] Clare received her name because of the last word of this prophecy.

In the year 1212, Saint Francis preached a series of sermons at the church of San Giorgio in Assisi. Clare, now 18, attended those sermons and wept. She secretly left her family and went to Francis. She took her vows before him and put herself under his direction. Her relatives found her and tried to persuade her to go home, but it was no use. She and a small group of women who had chosen her life of renunciation settled in a cottage next to the chapel of San Damiano. Thus the first community of Franciscan nuns was established.

Clare was one of the primary people who spread the Franciscan movement. The nuns practiced austerities unusual for women at that time. They slept on the ground, abstained from eating meat, went barefoot and spoke only when obliged to do so. Following Francis' rule that they own no property, they received all their material necessities and sustenance from alms. Because of her austerities, Clare was almost always sick and confined to her bed. Her illnesses continued for the last twenty-seven years of her life. Perhaps this teaches us somewhat of the dangers of extreme asceticism.

Clare's support of Saint Francis and his ministry was a large part of her mission. It was to Clare that Francis turned when in doubt, and it was she who urged him to continue his ministry to the people rather than lead a life of contemplation.

One author writes, "Clare was not only constant in work, she was frequent in prayer. It is told that she once stayed three days in a trance, and there is no doubt that she tasted the supreme bliss of the Heavenly Vision that is the crown and glory of the religious life. There are many legends about these later years that tell of her as the ecstatic—as the contemplative."[5] Clare died at the age of 60.

---

**LIFE NUMBER 11:** Place: Siena, Italy
Date: 1347 to 1380
Sex: Female

Catherine of Siena ranks among the greatest of Catholic mystics and spiritual writers. She was born the youngest of twenty-five children to a dyer in Siena, Italy. About the year 1354, she had a vision of Christ in glory. She vowed to remain a virgin. She devoted herself to Jesus, practicing austerities and spending many hours in prayer.

In 1366, when Catherine was 19 years old, as she prayed in the little room of her house where she had lived a secluded life for three years, Jesus promised her: "I will espouse you to me in faith"[6] and gave her a gold ring set with four pearls and a diamond. He said that this was her reward for scorning the vanities of the world and desiring only him.

In the spring of 1368, she received a vision of Christ and a command from him to "carry her love for Him out into the world and so give full scope to the charity within her."[7] She believed she was accepted as his bride and embarked on her active apostolate.

Catherine's life changed immediately, and she began a career of unceasing service. She left her cell to care for the poor and sick. She preached, traveled widely and addressed hundreds of letters to the prelates and sovereigns of her day, both advising and rebuking them. Wherever she went, she brought a spiritual revival.

She was instrumental in convincing Pope Gregory XI to leave Avignon, France, and return to Rome. (Since 1309, the Church had been headquartered in decadence at Avignon.) After he did so, she tried unsuccessfully to make peace between the Florentines and the Pope in order to keep the Church united. When her efforts failed, the Great Schism began. This was a thirty-year period in which there were two popes.

Catherine understood the true meaning of imitating the life of Christ, and in 1375 she received the stigmata, which was visible only to herself, enabling her to share in Christ's passion. Jesus taught Catherine that her bonding to him had to bear fruit not only for herself but for other souls as well. He said that she had to fly to heaven on "two wings": "love of me and love of your neighbor."[8]

In 1378, she dictated her "Dialogue," four treatises received under the inspiration of the Holy Ghost. The Catholic Church has recognized these writings as dictations from God to Saint Catherine. This is her spiritual testament to the world. Catherine died at the age of 33. She laid down her life for the Church, giving her body and her blood that the Church might survive.

When Jesus gave me the mantle of the Vicar of Christ for Church Universal and Triumphant in 1972, he said he gave it to me because I had understood as Catherine that you support whoever the pope is, whether he is good or evil, because you are supporting the office and the mantle. You do not go against the office and the mantle because its current occupant is not qualified or is in error. He said that because I was not attached to self but would always defend the mantle, whoever wore it, that he placed that mantle upon me.

---

**LIFE NUMBER 12:** Place: England
Date: 1505 to 1544
Sex: Female

Margaret More was the eldest child of Sir Thomas More. Thomas saw to it that his daughter was well-educated—far beyond the standards of the time for women. She learned Latin, Greek, mathematics, grammar and other subjects. She was More's favorite child and confidante. He called her Meg. She washed the hair shirt he secretly wore. She later preserved his unpublished writings.

King Henry VIII appointed Thomas More Chancellor of England. When More was in favor, the King was a frequent dinner guest. But Thomas quarreled with the King over the relaxation of heresy laws. He also refused to take the oath renouncing the pope's jurisdiction over the Church.

In April 1534, More was imprisoned in the Tower of London for refusal to take an oath of adherence to the act of succession that vested the crown in Anne Boleyn's issue. More's imprisonment brought severe economic hardship and loss of property to his family. In May of 1534, Meg visited her father in the Tower. She begged him to reconsider his action. He refused. He was indicted on July 1, 1535, tried and sentenced to death.

The following scene took place when Meg met her father on Tower Wharf after his trial (which she did not attend). First, he gave her his blessing. Then she "openly, in the sight of them all, embraced him, took him about the neck, and kissed him." He said: "Have patience, Margaret, and trouble not thyself. It is the will of God. Long hast thou known the secrets of my heart."[9]

While in prison, More exhibited remarkable composure and legendary good humor. On July 6, he was executed. Margaret took his headless torso for burial. His head was parboiled and exhibited on a stake on London Bridge. A year later, she bribed the executioner to give her father's head to her. She preserved it in spices until her death.

When I first contacted the records of this event in this life, I was still arguing with Thomas More, "Don't challenge the king. Don't allow yourself to be executed." I still could not understand why he did this. Of course, I did understand in my soul, but I was contacting those records of this very painful parting of the daughter with the father.

What I realized as I look back upon this life is that it prepared me for the ultimate sacrifice. It prepared me for embodiments that followed where I was to be assassinated or guillotined or meet an untimely death. It prepared me to be a messenger. It prepared me to stand on principles. It was a bonding of my heart to the heart of El Morya, who was embodied as Saint Thomas More.

I learned from him non-attachment. He instructed me by his martyrdom, his bravery. His example has never left me. I think it is the embodiment that moves me the most, although many of these move me for my memories with those who are now ascended masters. It was an amazing experience to be the daughter of Thomas More. He is probably the greatest father I have known from that time to the present.

---

**LIFE NUMBER 13:** Place: Austria and France
Date: 1755 to 1793
Sex: Female

Marie Antoinette, Queen of France, was born November 2, 1755, at Vienna, the eleventh daughter of Maria Theresa and Emperor Francis I. You may know of the tales of the great power and force of Maria Theresa. She was a very strong-willed woman, and she dominated her husband, Francis.

One day I was meditating upon this embodiment and I remembered an experience of what I was thinking about when I was in her womb. It was annoying me that she was disdainful, talking down to my father. I did not like the idea that she was overpowering him and putting him down and taking his power. That was my observation on the scene.

Of course, in those days, there wasn't much time spent by monarchs with their children. At age 15, she was married to the dauphin, the grandson of France's King Louis XV. From the very first, she was caught in court intrigue. Her marriage had been arranged by those who wanted to cement an alliance with Austria. The faction of the French court that did not want the alliance opposed Marie Antoinette from the beginning.

When she was 19, Louis XV died and her husband ascended the throne as Louis XVI. Marie Antoinette lived a life of pleasure and extravagance, but she had an obvious disregard of court etiquette that shocked many people.

She had enjoyed an informal upbringing at the relaxed court of Austria and was unprepared for her duties as Queen of France. Her husband was indifferent toward her. She was generally unpopular among the French people. But this was often due to pamphlets circulated against her and against the king. And it is generally known that the peasants and the people outside of Paris were more favorable toward the king and queen than those in the city.

In 1785, the incident called the Affair of the Diamond Necklace began. The queen was unfairly accused of an immoral relationship with a cardinal. This discredited the monarchy and finally destroyed the queen's reputation with the French people. Popular agitators accused her of having made the comment about the poor, "If they have no bread, let them eat cake." As far as historians can determine, she never said this. In fact, she was charitable to the poor.

On July 14, 1789, a mob stormed the fortress prison of the Bastille in the center of Paris, the beginning of the French Revolution. At this point Louis XVI lost his authority. On October 6, 1789, the royal family was pressured by angry mobs to move from Versailles to the Tuileries in Paris. Through secret emissaries, Marie Antoinette implored her brother to send an army to rescue her family. After two years, help still had not arrived, so the royal family decided to leave France.

On June 20, 1791, the family disguised themselves as commoners and attempted to escape from Paris. They were discovered at Varennes, captured and forced to return to Paris, where they were closely guarded. In January 1793, Louis XVI was executed. In October 1793, Marie Antoinette was tried before the Revolutionary Tribunal and found guilty. On October 16, 1793, she was guillotined.

I had the recall of this life when I was studying French history in college. When I read about the flight to Varennes and the attempted escape of the king and queen, I knew that I was in that carriage. I could hear the horses. I could hear the man in his store. I could hear the entire scene. And I said, "Either I was the driver or the maid or the queen or the king or somebody, but I was there. I was one of the people in that scene."

My recollection of these events since that time is an amazing one. I remember being imprisoned for a number of years. The story goes that she was once served on a giant silver platter with a cover on it the head of her lady-in-waiting. Many cruelties and brutalities were practiced against her. She was not well.

She rode in the cart to the guillotine. The Comte de Saint Germain was seen by Madame d'Adhemar, the author of the diary that was excerpted in the book *The Count of Saint Germain*, by Isabel Cooper-Oakley, at La Place de la Révolution at the guillotining of Marie Antoinette. The master stood with Portia beneath the statue of the Goddess of Liberty that had recently been erected in the square. Immediately following her execution, they took the soul of Marie Antoinette to the Cave of Light, the Great Divine Director's etheric retreat in India.

There are many different accounts of the life of the king and queen—some favorable, some not so favorable. We will see the end to this tale when I get to the end of these lifetimes.

---

**LIFE NUMBER 14:** Place: Austria
Date: 1837 to 1898
Sex: Female

Elisabeth Amalie Eugenie, Empress of Austria, was born December 24, 1837, at Possenhoffen Castle near Munich. She was the daughter of the Bavarian duke Maximilian Joseph. She received an unconventional education. She accompanied her eccentric father on hunting expeditions. She became an expert rider and climber.

In August 1853, she met her cousin, Emperor Franz Joseph I, ruler of Austria. He fell in love with her at first sight. He was 23, she was 15. They were married and she became Empress.

Life was difficult from the start. The emperor had numerous love affairs. His involvement in state business left him little time for Elisabeth. One of her confidantes wrote that he believed her to be "too young, too inexperienced, and too indifferent to become his real companion and comrade."[10]

She bore four children—three daughters and a son. The first daughter died in infancy. The Archduchess, Franz-Joseph's mother, forbade her to raise her own children, claiming she was only a child herself.

Her exceptional beauty, charm and generosity made her popular with her subjects. But her impatience with the Viennese court etiquette, her love for horsemanship and frequent visits to the imperial riding school scandalized Austrian high society. She exhibited great compassion for the common people and tended the wounded during the Seven Weeks War. She began to spend more time away from court.

In November 1860, she separated from her husband over his infidelities. They were estranged for seven years. She spent this time traveling and learning Latin and Greek. She involved herself in state affairs on behalf of the people of Hungary. She learned the Magyar language and helped to arrange the Compromise of 1867, which raised Hungary to equal status with Austria in the empire. She was also involved in charitable work. In 1889, her only son, the Crown Prince Archduke Rudolf, committed suicide. Elisabeth never fully recovered from this shock.

On September 10, 1898, she was assassinated by the Italian anarchist Luigi Luccheni while visiting Geneva, Switzerland. She was walking from her hotel to a steamer on the lake when she was stabbed. At Luccheni's trial, he stated that human suffering was the motive for his act and that he had no regrets. He said, "When I heard those bells [announcing her death] I considered them to be the funeral knell of the bourgeoisie, whom I detest."[11]

She is remembered as being independent, unconventional and high-spirited and possessed of exceptional intelligence and kindness.

## An Ancient Karma

When I was 17, I walked in the very places where Elisabeth of Austria was in Geneva. I stood at the place where this anarchist drove a carefully filed piece of metal into her heart. Despite this mortal wound, she walked onto the boat and laid down, finally passing a few hours later.

The Hapsburgs' clothing was on display in the Metropolitan Museum of Art, in New York, a number of years ago. They had a mannequin wearing the dress she was wearing when she was assassinated. I approached the dress and there was a tiny hole over the heart where the instrument had gone through that dress.

I believe that I have met all of these characters in this life, including those who surrounded Marie Antoinette and Elisabeth of Austria. I have met some of them in very personal ways and some in passing. And wherever there was karma, I had to balance that karma.

I have told you about three different deaths—the assassination of Nefertiti, the guillotining of Marie Antoinette, the stabbing of Elisabeth of Austria. However, what we are not seeing is many, many other lifetimes. The Karmic Board has given me the opportunity to be in embodiment almost continuously, with very little time out of embodiment, to be sure that I would be ready for this life and this mission and all that we would have to do.

I think that there probably have been plenty of other embodiments that ended in this type of death. I have also recognized that in this life I seem to have what has always followed me: many people who love me and many people who hate me. I don't seem to draw any neutrals in this matter. People polarize very quickly. I have asked myself, of course, aside from the fallen angels and reprobate ones who could not be converted back to God and who have made themselves my enemies, why have people hated me? Why have they really hated me in other embodiments?

I asked El Morya to please give me an understanding of this. And I have that record, which has just come to me in the past couple of weeks. It gives me the profound understanding of where I have been all of these centuries.

Where did my karma come from? Where did I make this karma of being vulnerable to assassination and people's hatred? This is the second embodiment, which I have saved for the end.

---

**LIFE NUMBER 2:** Place: Atlantis
Date: c. 25,000 BC
Sex: Female

It is Atlantis about 25,000 BC, which puts this 27,000 years ago. It was a time of decline in that civilization. I became a queen, ruling over much of the continent. I began with good intentions and was benevolent at first. I wanted to make people do what was best for themselves and each other. I established laws about dress, moral conduct, family responsibility, alcohol consumption. I also established laws forbidding usury, slave trafficking, unfair business practices, racketeering and mistreatment of workers.

In the beginning, the common people praised the laws because they thought they would get a better shake. But the penalties were harsh and they were carried out without mercy. The people then turned against me and my laws. To counteract that, I did what the rulers of the time did. I had a network of spies that carried out assassinations of those who opposed me. Many people were executed for the sins of adultery, drunkenness, stealing, and so on. I hoped against hope that the people might be convinced to change their ways once they discovered that I was in earnest and that I would not bend on the reforms. But this did not happen. Instead they rioted.

I was asked to step down by the nation's council of elders for the sake of national unity. I abdicated and lived the rest of my life in exile. But I had made a karma that I would have to balance in succeeding lives. I wish to tell you that not until this lifetime did I finally balance this karma. I am very grateful to be able to give you this record today.

Sometimes reporters and others have asked me, "Why are you always somebody important or a queen or something in your past lives?" I tell them I wasn't certainly always such. We have many dips in our sine wave of embodiments, and they cover the lowest and the highest in terms of our station in life. But one of the reasons I have been a queen on a number of occasions is because I have queen karma. And there is only one way to balance queen karma—you have to come back and be a queen again.

So this is that point of origin 27,000 years ago. I would have to contact many people and I would have to give to them the complete balancing of whatever happened to them in that life, whether they were assassinated, whether they were killed or whether they were simply deprived or mistreated or whatever. This could take a long, long time, depending on how long such things had been going on.

I want to comment about this embodiment in conclusion. I can feel in the record in my own soul that there came a time, after many, many, many thousands of years of having gone forth to bring these reprobate ones back to God, that I was no longer reacting to them from the centeredness of God-manifestation. Their rejection of God and his message and his Law and his teaching was causing me to become more and more angry inside that I couldn't woo them back to God. So now I was going to create a situation where they, in order to survive and to live, would have to obey these laws whereby they would be on the side of right.

The interesting thing is that in the teachings of Phylos the Tibetan we find that the Rai of the Suernis, Rai Ernon, was the one who forced his people into a certain moral code and a certain standard of preserving the sacred fire. And the people hated him—to the last man. He spoke about this, saying that it is the absolute conclusion of the ascended masters that you cannot force laws, morals, standards, honor, a spiritual path or a spiritual discipline upon anyone.[12]

You can set the example. You can give the teaching. You can urge them. You can preach to them. You can love them. You can do everything that you can possibly do. But you cannot force an individual, a people, a nation, a church to do something because you say it is true, even if it is true. The greatest of ascended masters bow to the light within us and they withdraw when we do not receive from them their teaching.

In a very small scale you can apply this lesson to your own life. Your husband, your wife, your children, your relatives do not have to be students of the ascended masters. They may very well make it to heaven without being students of the ascended masters. The important thing is that you should not worry about them and burden yourself. You should be an example, a living example of the Path and the teaching and an example of love. Some will receive you and love you. Some will hate you. You just be that teaching, but don't try to force it on anyone.

There has been a great mellowing in my heart through all the ages. In a few of these embodiments, you can see my deep desire to serve Jesus Christ and Saint Francis and many who were a part of the brothers and sisters. And surely it has been my desire to see the preservation of the Catholic Church. In this lifetime, I was born outside of the Church, but with a great love for Mother Mary and the saints. And I realize that God did not allow me to be born in that church because I had already given my life to it, and I must go outside it to preach the Word of God.

Mother Mary's appearance at Knock with John the Beloved and Saint Joseph is striking because it was an appearance in which she was standing outside of the church, not inside the church.[13] It showed me that she was coming to the people directly and bypassing the hierarchy. And so often she appears to children because they are receptive.

## The Voice of God

We can see in these embodiments of mine and of those whose stories preceded this that it has taken most of the people to come to this day and age about 30,000 years since their karma began or thereabouts. And if I didn't give a lifetime that far back for some people, you can be sure that they had one.

I hope that this lecture has brought to you a real depth of soul-understanding for your own life and for your own actions. I hope I have convinced you that karma is a reality and perhaps I might even have convinced you that reincarnation is a reality.

Prior to this incarnation, I asked for my karma at birth and

I received it. And I was aware that I was surrounded by many burdens in the first 18 years of my life. But as I look back, I am absolutely certain that every single person who came into my life was some karmic situation that needed to be settled. It was not an easy life, but I walked with God as I walked with my understanding of God through Christian Science. And I had great experiences of light.

When it came time to leave my home at age 18, I asked God what he had placed there for me. The voice spoke clearly in my heart and in my mind to take down the book *The I AM Discourses* that was on my mother's shelf and read it. I opened the book and saw the portrait of Saint Germain, and I was electrified. I realized later that Saint Germain was standing right there. But I could not see him because of the very, very dense food that I had eaten in the tradition of my parents' cooking. Yet I was aware, I was electrified, and my inner being knew that I had to find him.

Many years later, reflecting on that moment, he made a comment to me that was very interesting, which I think all of us could take to heart. He said, "You had 18 years as an indentured servant, so to speak, and you had to serve these parents and serve all the people you knew and help all the people you helped."

I never stopped helping people—friends, neighbors, schoolmates, anyone. Whatever people needed, I would help them. It was a life of service and it was a difficult situation. But Saint Germain said that I had behaved as a chela* in respecting my parents. Even if their behavior was not always respectable, I respected their office. I was obedient to them and I did not challenge them.

Saint Germain was saying that I had passed my tests, balanced the karma I was intended to balance in that town and in that situation. Had I not done so, he would not have come to me at the age of 18 in answer to my prayer, to quicken me and show

***Chela* is the term in the East for the student of a spiritual teacher or guru.

me the book and his portrait in that book, and to give me that impetus for the quest of finding him personally.

Saint Germain came to the court of Louis XVI and Marie Antoinette to warn Louis XVI of the coming revolution. Louis XVI listened to his advisors and not to Saint Germain, but on numerous occasions Marie Antoinette was present when the Count Saint Germain came to converse with the king. So there was a very direct memory of Saint Germain in that life and other past lives.

I am devoted to Saint Germain with all of my heart because I remember how gracious he has been to me in so many lifetimes. And the same is true of so many ascended masters.

In conclusion, I advise you again to listen to the voice of God in your heart. Don't ever be afraid to obey the voice of God within, because it will always lead you back to him and never lead you astray. No matter how odd or how funny it might seem, listen to that voice. Know it is God's voice. And when you know it is God's voice, follow it. And don't ever be afraid to give of yourself to people, to those around you.

CHAPTER 11

# Where Do We Go from Here?

When she was 16, Rachel Morris* almost killed her father. The abuse had started when she was little, when she used to sit on his knee while he combed her soft, curly hair into ringlets. But then he wanted to do more than play. And he said he would kill her and her mother if she ever told anyone. So she never did.

But she used to wake up screaming, "No, Daddy!" Her mother never said anything. And Rachel grew up playing strange games by herself out under the oak tree of their white frame home in suburban Illinois. She buried her Barbie dolls in carefully lined shoeboxes, marking their graves with pebble outlines. She would dig them up the next day and repeat the ritual.

When she was 16, Rachel stayed out late one summer evening, walking and holding hands with Rick Alisandretti from geometry class. As she opened the screened door, a painted china dog flew past her and crashed on the faded porch wood. "Where have

*"Rachel" is a composite character whose story comes out of my counseling work.

you been?" Before she could make it up the stairs to her room, Daddy had slapped her face, hard, torn her white blouse and sent one of the praying hands bookends sailing past her ear. "Don't ever let me catch you with a boy again! I'll kill him! And I'll kill you, too!"

When Rachel tiptoed down the steps later that night, powder-blue suitcase in hand, she could hear Daddy snoring in the living room. She went into the kitchen and slowly opened the glass-knobbed drawer. Daddy always kept the carving knives sharp. She stared at them and at her shadow, the moonlight throwing the image of her bobbed hair large against the wall in front of her.

She sighed, quietly closed the drawer, picked up her suitcase and eased herself out the back door. She never saw her father again. She went to Chicago, waitressed her way through college and was hired at an investment firm. Although she advanced quickly in her career, she knew she hadn't gotten beyond her past.

Rachel spent one day a month "sick," crying in the closet and thinking about the dead Barbie dolls. A string of relationships ended in failure, and at 35, she found herself alone. She was first able to talk about her past to a therapist, looking out of his Wacker Drive office onto Lake Michigan. After a year in which she told every detail of her past, looking for keys that would help her get beyond the memories, she felt stuck.

Why had all this happened to her? Why was she born with an abusive father and a mother who let him abuse her? What did she do to deserve it? Deep down inside, she felt it must be something terrible.

As she drifted along the sidewalk, lost in thought, someone stuffed a violet handbill into her hand. "Learn to use the violet flame to transmute painful memories," it said. It was an advertisement for one of my lectures. Rachel attended and listened to me explain how to use the violet flame—a technique that combines visualization and the repeating of rhythmic prayers called "decrees" to call forth the violet frequency of God's light. This light energy has the special quality of erasing and changing negative aspects of ourselves. I call it "transmutation." Mystics throughout the ages have known how to use this energy. But it wasn't taught publicly until the 1930s, when Guy and Edna Ballard founded the "I AM Movement." Mark Prophet showed me how to use it when I began working with him in 1961.

During the lecture, Rachel sat towards the back listening to my explanations and reading the decrees carefully. She kept silent as the group repeated them, not sure she wanted to join in. The first time Rachel used the violet flame, she was sitting forward in an olive-green armchair in the living room of her Lincoln Park apartment, feet on a stack of *Vogues,* looking at a framed Georgia O'Keeffe lithograph.

She held the booklet six inches away from her face and began to repeat:

> I AM the Violet Flame in action in me now
> I AM the Violet Flame to Light alone I bow
> I AM the Violet Flame in mighty Cosmic Power
> I AM the Light of God shining every hour
> I AM the Violet Flame blazing like a sun
> I AM God's sacred power freeing every one.

Such a simple rhyme, she thought. Like a nursery rhyme. She remembered that I had explained that "I AM" means "God in me is." Each time we repeat "I AM the Violet Flame," we are liberating a part of ourselves to be one with the part of ourselves that is God.

She repeated it nine times and then went to bed. The next night at the same time, she tried it again. After a few repetitions she was able to remember the verse and so she closed her eyes. She got the impression of a shower of light falling around her. After she finished, she felt a tingly feeling all over. After two weeks of giving violet-flame decrees, she felt more at peace with herself, but she was still troubled by painful flashbacks from the past.

One night she had a vivid dream. She saw an image of a black, high-laced boot planting itself in a mud puddle. Raindrops pelted her back and made the puddles dance. She walked slowly toward a two-story, Tudor-style house up the road. She could feel the rain soaking through her clothes and trickling down her back, but she simply pulled forward her black poke bonnet and walked as slowly as possible. As she lifted the wooden beam of the gate and went in the back door, Mr. Farnsworth was waiting.

She flashed on another scene: her sobbing and him laughing. Her threatening never to come back. Him threatening to turn her family out of their cottage. Her slashing his throat with a kitchen knife as he slept. Her running away to London, later dying in a cold garret.

When she woke up, she could remember the dream, smell the English countryside, hear the rain splashing in the puddles as she walked toward the house. But she felt lighter and freer, almost as if the rain had washed away the feelings of the past. "Why should I feel so good after such an awful dream?" she asked herself.

Several months later I had a chance to meet her and she told me about her dream and her painful childhood. I explained to her that she had remembered a past life and that it contained karmic seeds of her current life challenges. Mr. Farnsworth had reincarnated as her father and she had balanced her karma for killing him by being reborn as his daughter. She had broken the karmic cycle by not taking the opportunity to kill him again.

But recalling the karmic record was just the first step in getting beyond her past. She still had spiritual work to do. The memory of the violence, the pain, the grief and the guilt were holding her back from getting on with her life plan. On a spiritual level the energy that had gone into those emotions had solidified around her soul like black tar.

The violet flame can dissolve "misqualified" energy. It is a spiritual solvent that God has given us to dissolve that "hardened" energy and liberate ourselves from destructive patterns.

"But why was I shown this past life now?" asked Rachel.

"Your soul was ready to deal with the record," I answered. "That's why I recommend using the violet flame rather than hypnotherapy to look into past lives. With regression therapy, you may come upon all kinds of memories, some not even your own, that can confuse you and lead you off on tangents. With the violet flame, you know that God will reveal to you only as much as you are ready to deal with."

"What am I supposed to do with this dream?"

"The dream was given to you so that you could dissolve the karmic records with the violet flame."

"How do I do that?"

"As you give the violet flame, the scenes from the dream will come up on the screen of your mind. Every time you see those scenes, visualize a giant eraser, like a chalkboard eraser, only violet, rubbing away the picture. After you do this enough times, the memory will stop being painful and gradually fade from the forefront of your mind."

"I'll try it," she said. "I'll try anything at this point."

A few weeks later, Rachel called me. She sounded excited. "I had the most amazing experience! It was just after I finished giving my violet-flame decrees. All of these pictures flooded my mind. I could see what happened to me after I died in that London garret. My body seemed to be light. It floated up into a beam of light. I heard a sound like wind and then felt myself pulled upwards. I was in a beautiful place with gardens and flowers, and I just stayed there for a while and played with children."

"Good! You're starting to get beyond the record. Now you need to ask God to reveal to you the next record you need to work on to get on with your life plan."

"What is my life plan?" asked Rachel.

"Your life plan is something that is prepared in the period between one life and the next. Have you heard about the 'life review' that people often go through during near-death experiences?"

"Yes."

"The beings who conduct the review are ascended masters, souls who have balanced their karma and achieved reunion with God. There are usually seven but the numbers vary, depending on the needs of the soul.

"After the review, they prepare a plan for your next life based on what you did—positive or negative—in your preceding lives. They tell you that you will be put into a situation where you have to meet karmic challenges. If you pass them, you get to go on to the next level of challenges. If you stumble over an obstacle—if you had killed your father or even killed yourself out of guilt feelings—you would have had to come back to face the same obstacle again."

Rachel and I had several more conversations. She began to feel lighter about her past. She was able to visit her mother, talk to her about the abuse and to forgive her for not intervening. She no longer gets debilitated by painful flashbacks from the past. And she is more positive about the future. Although her story isn't neatly wrapped up in a wedding dress, she has attracted a relationship with a strong and caring man.

## So What If I've Lived Before?

Many people, after hearing about reincarnation, ask what the point of it all is. The answer is nothing and everything. The point of reincarnation is not to remember that you were Charlemagne or Napoleon or Cleopatra. And it's not to get caught up in fantasy about fencing in sixteenth-century France or sailing with the Vikings. The reason you should be interested in your past lives today is that knowing about them helps you deal with your karma.

There are several ways of learning about past lives, not all of them safe. If you use hypnotherapy, drugs or regression to recall past lives, you run the risk of being introduced to your karma prematurely—before you are ready to deal with it. There may be other more important karmas that you need to balance first. I would not recommend that you try a clairvoyant—they vary in skill and their past life readings are often inaccurate.

The safest way to recall past lives is to give decrees to the violet flame. But remember that recalling a past life is not something to be taken lightly. When you become aware of it, the karma of that life comes to the surface. It's like opening a can of worms. You can't do anything else until you clean up the mess. So the only thing to do is to roll up your sleeves, make calls to the violet flame each day and spend your time in serving life. It can take as little as six months of concentrated work and decrees to balance the karma of one past life.

You may even be able to watch the violet flame in action. To people who have developed their spiritual sight, the violet flame actually looks like fire—in colors ranging from dark indigo to brilliant amethyst to a violet-pink. The ancient alchemists tried to change, or transmute, base metals into gold. The violet flame is the true alchemist's tool because it actually changes the molecular structure of your karmic patterns—and that's why I call it the violet *transmuting* flame.

As you give the violet flame, frames and glyphs of past lives may come before your mind. You may see yourself as you were in ages long past. Or you may just have the impression that you were in a particular time or place. If the records are painful—and they usually are because your soul is crying out for resolution—you may feel sadness or regret. But you will also feel liberated because you know that as you give your violet-flame decrees, you are clearing the records of your past karma.

There are two elements you are transmuting when you use

the violet flame. The first is the emotional and soul memory of the events that are causing you pain. And the second is the karmic energy that binds you to those you have hurt or who have hurt you. I like to call this the "cause, effect, record and memory" of karma, which includes all energy that you have tied up or wasted in anger, sadness or worry about the past.

Past-life records are like files on your computer. You need to erase the negative records and memories in order to make room for positive programming. As you do so through the violet flame, you are freeing your soul to move on to higher levels of existence.

There are two ways of erasing, or clearing, your karmic debts: service and prayer. Service is helping, supporting and loving the one you have wronged. If you are not in contact with that person (if they are deceased or you don't know where they are or you are not on speaking terms), you can clear your debt with them by offering violet-flame decrees on their behalf. You can also balance karma by helping other people who are in need, even if you have no karma with them at all.

Psychotherapy may give you keys to understanding yourself and to making better choices in your life. And it can give you resolution with your past. But it does not transmute the cause, effect, record and memory of those painful incidents. This will remain with you until you clear it by service, prayer and violet-flame decrees.

You may gain resolution with someone you know because you've seen the record of the past and you've decided to make it positive in this life. But that record won't go away until you learn how to use the sacred fire of the Holy Spirit to erase it. And it is only by getting beyond those records that, like Rachel, you can clear the way for your soul to receive new opportunities that may not even have been written into your life plan. You can accelerate your soul's progress in this life and thus make your way more quickly to the goal of divine union.

Each time you balance the karma of a certain lifetime, God

may then reveal to you the next most important life that you need to tackle. And the next and the next. It's important not to feel burdened by the record of a past life. We have all made mistakes in the past or we wouldn't be here today. Forgive yourself and move on. Be grateful that you are here and that you have the opportunity to erase those records with the violet flame.

Once you start, keep on going. One step begins the trek of a thousand miles. Each time you go through a past life with the violet flame, you gain a new sense of your soul's liberation. And by and by you realize that you are taking command of your soul's destiny.

## Free Will and Karma

Your life plan is not set in stone from the minute you are born. There are preprogrammed forks in the road, and the outcome of your life depends on your choices.

You can look at life a little like a very complex computer game. Your karmic challenges are determined by your past actions. Get over the hurdles, and you advance. You get new talents. Each battle you win is another step on the road to the grand prize: union with God. You learn to love someone who has done something terrible to you. Advance one level. You help someone you wronged in the past. Advance another level.

You take revenge on someone who has hurt you. A gate closes, you must take the long road around, and maybe you fail to meet up with the person who holds the key to your next task.

There is a fine balance between free will and karmic destiny. Your karma is your destiny because you have written the script in previous lives. But the final outcome will depend on the choices you make in this life and what you do when confronted with the challenges of that destiny. And you can also change the script by balancing your karma ahead of time through the violet flame and through making right choices.

The kind of cosmic computer that can keep track of all of

these choices and records for millions of different people almost defies imagination. But the real computer is the infinite mind of God. Today we have computers that can keep track of millions of telephone calls every minute. If we can conceive of this, then we can imagine that God and his emissaries, all one with the Infinite, can also keep track of our progress here on earth.

Earth is a schoolroom, as Origen of Alexandria believed and as Mark Prophet was fond of saying. And we can't get out of it until we pass our tests, make the grade and graduate. But it's a closed-book test. We can't peek at the answers until the test is over. If we fail the test, we have to start all over.

Psychologists who have worked with past-life regression have found over and over again that there are karmic tests that are part of each individual's life plan. Dr. Joel Whitton, a Toronto psychiatrist who works with past-life regression, found that the better we perform on these tests, the faster we progress in this life. In their book *Life Between Life,* Whitton and Joe Fisher tell the story of Steve Logan, a man who "felt extremely negative" toward his father, who lived in a Miami nursing home.

One day, although he rarely visited his father, he followed a prompting and stopped by. His father was connected to various life-support devices, including a respirator. As he stood alone in the room, write Whitton and Fisher, Steve noticed that the respirator tube was no longer connected and his father was having a hard time breathing.

This situation presented Steve with a dilemma: he could either call a nurse to save his father's life or he could turn a blind eye and allow him to die. After a moment's reflection, he ran from the room shouting for a nurse who hastily replaced the tube.

Some years later, at the age of twenty-nine, Steve had a serious bicycle accident in a small town in Oregon. He was hit broadside by a truck and was considered very lucky to escape with a fractured femur.

When Steve was in his early forties, he underwent hypnosis and learned that the two incidents were karmically related. According to his karmic script, his fate in the bicycle accident was to be determined by his response to his father's plight. By making the decision to save his father's life, he had changed the outcome of the bicycle accident. "If I could forgive him his transgressions against me—which appeared to extend over several lifetimes—I would not be killed in the bicycle accident," said Steve.

"The expectation was there in the plan that because of my past conduct I would allow my father to die. But I passed the test and, after my accident, the plan was at an end! I learned that sketchy plans for future lives had been brought forward to operate in the current life."[1]

You never know how a service that you render another can help your own soul. This story reminds us not to pass up an opportunity to help someone in need. I can remember one day when I was nineteen and I was working at the United Nations. I was standing on a street corner in New York, on my way to work, waiting for the light to change.

Standing in front of me was an elderly man, somewhat disheveled. He stepped down from the curb right into the path of a car that came speeding around the corner. In about two seconds, he would be hit and killed.

It was a moment in eternity. I looked at the car, I looked at the man. I grabbed his coat from behind the neck and picked him right up (he was just a sliver of a man) and lifted him onto the sidewalk. The car sped by and his little unshaven face turned around and looked up at me and said through missing teeth, "Gee, tanks, miss!" The funny thing about it was that everyone else on the street corner saw him but no one else did anything about it.

It was a moving experience as well as a lesson in karma and free will. My saving him was not preordained. I could have chosen not to do it. The opportunity was written in my life plan, but my reaction was not.

## Choosing Your Life

These episodes demonstrate the interplay between karma and free will. There's a lot of talk in New Age circles about "choosing" lives: "I *chose* to be an actress in this life." But would anyone really choose to be born to abusive parents, to be poor if they could choose to be rich, to be ugly if they could choose to be beautiful? If we really "choose" our lots in life, we should all be walking around looking like gods and goddesses. The answer is a little more complicated than that. We "choose" our lives, but only within narrow borders that are dictated by our karma.

Plato gave a good explanation. In *The Republic,* he wrote that souls do "choose" their lives, but their time on earth is lengthened or shortened depending on their choice.[2] Therefore they will be more likely to "choose" a life that results in soul progress rather than a life that is simply pleasant. A soul who spent one life in a beautiful body may "choose" an ugly one the next time because his karma dictates that he learn to go beyond appearances and to develop compassion.

These life choices are made in conjunction with the group of ascended masters I told Rachel about. They review our lives with us and show us what we did right, what we did wrong, what tests we passed, what grades we got and what tests we failed. And then they tell us what we will have to do when we reincarnate to complete those tests and assignments. They tell us the karmic relationships we will have in our lives, and many times these are with our family members.

Parents often represent your primary karma. They are the first thing on your karmic plate in this life, so to speak, and until you get beyond them, you can't advance to the next level in your life plan.

We spend a lot of time today thinking about our parents. People say, "If only my parents had given me music lessons when I wanted them, I might be a concert pianist today." "If only Mom and Dad had gotten along better, I might be more successful in my relationships." But the most important thing to remember about your parents is that they brought you into this world. You are flesh of their flesh. They gave you a body so that you could pass your karmic tests in this life and make spiritual progress. There are no perfect parents. We need to love them, to learn what we can from them and then to move on.

The message that comes across from the findings of past-life and inter-life regression is: You alone are responsible for who and what you are today. If you don't like who you are, you can do something about it. And the circumstances of your life are designed to help you do just that.

So if you are sitting on earth in an underprivileged body or in an unloved body or if you can't attract the kind of friends you want, don't blame it on anyone else. Get to work on yourself. You are not limited by your genetic material or the circumstances of your birth. You can transcend yourself every day. You can access talents you have stored up in heavenly treasure houses. Your talents are the accumulation of hard work, ingenuity and your desire to improve your lot.

Once you have determined that you are going to balance your karma in this life and return to God, you can sometimes sneak a peek at your life challenges. This may happen while you are meditating or giving the violet flame, or even as a vivid impression left in your mind when you awaken—suddenly you will get a "preview" of your life to come. If this hasn't happened to you, just ask God and the angels to show you where you are in your life plan and what you need to work on. The answer won't be long in coming.

The violet flame is a great gift from God, and I hope you

enjoy experimenting with it. Whether you are part of organized religion or you use a combination of spiritual practices, you can add the violet flame to your daily rituals. You will see that it can be a valuable tool—one that can make the difference in the "great combat" of life, which is really about defeating those negative parts of our lives that we have created in the past.

CHAPTER 12

# The Violet Flame

The Apostle John, the messenger of Jesus, declared the Lord's message: "God is Light, and in him is no darkness at all.... If we walk in the Light, as he is in the Light, we have fellowship one with another, and the blood of Jesus Christ his Son cleanseth us from all sin."[1]

John saw the violet light, he declared the violet light, and he walked in the violet light. He knew the violet light to be the essence of the Body and Blood of Christ. And he knew the violet flame as that all-consuming fire that transmutes the cause and core of sin and the karma that is the record of and the penalty for that sin.

(And if you ask me how I know, I will tell you that I have seen in the akashic record Jesus using the violet flame in his healings and miracles and initiating his closest disciple, John, in its use.)

The saints robed in white who gather before the Lamb and the throne of God also testify that they have washed their robes in the violet flame.[2] And every lifestream who has returned to the Source has engaged in the seventh-ray ablution—the ritual of bathing body and soul, mind and heart in the violet flame. They have washed and scrubbed, washed and scrubbed their four lower bodies, singing with the violet singing flame all the way Home!

The violet flame is the gift of the Holy Spirit that comes to us under the sponsorship of the ascended master Saint Germain, who reintroduced the knowledge of the violet flame to the world in the twentieth century. Not since the early days of Atlantis when its golden-age civilization was at its height have mankind had access to the alchemy of the violet flame. It was withdrawn when the priesthood and the public alike began the misuse and the disuse of the Unfed Flame on the temple altar, compromising its seventh-ray aspect, the violet flame, as well.

With the sinking of Atlantis, the mystery schools and retreats of the adepts were removed to the Himalayas or transferred to the etheric octave. Thereafter the knowledge of the violet flame—how to invoke it, how to apply it in the alchemy of the seventh ray—was handed down from master to disciple until Saint Germain released it to the world in the 1930s. And today the master's students on every continent give gratitude to God for the *joie de vivre* and the positive spin they get each time they give a violet-flame decree.

The violet flame is the key to individual and world transmutation. It works in microcosmic and macrocosmic worlds, from the smallest particle of matter to molecule to mind to materialization in man and mundane circles.

In his book *The Chela and the Path,* El Morya explains the origin and nature of the violet flame:

> The violet flame comes forth from the violet ray, that aspect of the white light that is called the seventh ray. It is indeed the seventh-ray aspect of the Holy Spirit. Just as the sunlight passing through a prism is refracted into the rainbow of the seven color rays, so through the

> consciousness of the Holy Spirit the light of the Christ is refracted for mankind's use in the planes of Matter.
>
> Each of the seven rays is a concentrated, activating force of the light of God having a specific color and frequency. Each ray can also manifest as a flame of the same color and vibration. The application of the flame results in a specific action of the Christ in body and soul, mind and heart.[3]

How does a ray become a flame, and specifically how does the violet ray become the violet flame? When you invoke the violet flame, it comes forth from the heart of your I AM Presence as a ray of light that is violet in color. That ray descends like a powerful sunbeam from its source in the Great Central Sun to what is called the plane of invocation. Wherever you may be in the universe, in whatever socket of consciousness you find yourself, the level from which you invoke the light of God is defined as the plane of invocation.

An invocation is a call to light that is transmitted from your heart to the heart of God instantaneously. The response comes forth on the return current. When the violet ray descends from your I AM Presence to the plane of invocation, a violet flame springs up. Simply put, the flame is an intensification of a light ray that has been stepped up by the fervor of your heart's call and the zeal of the Lord's response. The phenomenon brings to mind the physical counterpart: a ray of light from the sun passed through a magnifying glass causing an object to burst into flame.

When you invoke the violet flame for the healing of a specific problem, this is how it works. It envelops each atom of your being individually. Instantaneously a polarity is set up between the nucleus of the atom (which, being Matter, assumes the negative pole) and the white-fire core of the flame (which, being Spirit, assumes the positive pole).

The dual action of the light in the nucleus of the atom and the light in the enveloping violet flame establishes an oscillation that causes the untransmuted densities to be dislodged from between the electrons. As this substance is loosened, at non-physical, or "meta-physical," dimensions of Matter, the electrons begin to vibrate with an increased amount of energy, throwing the misqualified substance into the violet flame.

On contact with this fiery essence of freedom's flame, the misqualified energy is transmuted and God's energy is restored to its native purity. Relieved of the patterns of imperfection and restored to the plus-minus balance of Alpha and Omega, this energy of the Holy Spirit is returned to the individual's causal body, where it is stored until he elects to use it once again to bring forth the noble work of the Christ "on earth as it is in heaven."

This alchemy takes place on the material plane, though not necessarily in the objective "physical" plane; for every atom of substance has its counterpart in the astral, mental and etheric compartments of the Matter universe as well as in the spiritual octaves of light.

The violet flame can alter, mitigate or entirely turn back prophecy. When you invoke the violet flame in the name of your mighty I AM Presence and Holy Christ Self through the heart of Jesus Christ and Saint Germain, angels of the seventh ray direct it into the density and discord that characterizes the out-of-alignment state of our people and our planet.

Indeed, old age, disease and death are the result of mankind's misapplication of the universal laws of God's harmony. Through giving daily decrees to the violet flame, these conditions can be forestalled, and the quality of life can be greatly enhanced. Give the elderly a good diet and a daily dose of the violet flame and they would walk, skip and jog right up out of their convalescent homes!

The best way for you to understand the violet flame is to see for yourself what it does! Therefore I would like to invite you to experiment with these violet-flame decrees along with the thoughtforms for meditation and visualization. And I urge you to prove what great good you can accomplish for yourself and the world through the ever-widening circle of your aura.

It doesn't matter what your religion or philosophy of life is, because the violet flame belongs to all people. Anyone can take the dynamic decrees to the violet flame and use them to heal themselves and planet Earth.

---

**"Heart, Head and Hand Decrees"**
by El Morya

Violet Fire

*Heart*

Violet Fire, thou Love divine,
Blaze within this heart of mine!
Thou art Mercy forever true,
Keep me always in tune with you.

*Head*

I AM Light, thou Christ in me,
Set my mind forever free;
Violet Fire, forever shine
Deep within this mind of mine.

God who gives my daily bread,
With Violet Fire fill my head
Till thy radiance heavenlike
Makes my mind a mind of Light.

*Hand*

I AM the hand of God in action,
Gaining Victory every day;
My pure soul's great satisfaction
Is to walk the Middle Way.

Tube of Light

Beloved I AM Presence bright,
Round me seal your Tube of Light
From Ascended Master flame
Called forth now in God's own name.
Let it keep my temple free
From all discord sent to me.

I AM calling forth Violet Fire
To blaze and transmute all desire,
Keeping on in Freedom's name
Till I AM one with the Violet Flame.

Forgiveness

I AM Forgiveness acting here,
Casting out all doubt and fear,
Setting men forever free
With wings of cosmic Victory.

I AM calling in full power
For Forgiveness every hour;
To all life in every place
I flood forth forgiving grace.

As you recite these "Heart, Head and Hand Decrees," visualize taking place exactly what they say. Each word or phrase carries a thoughtform that you fill in with the fiat of your mind and heart as much as you do with your spoken word.

Visualize yourself surrounded by the violet flame. See the violet flame rising, pulsating in endless shades and gradations of purple-pink with violet hue and electric blue. By and by as we decree, the violet flame, rising up from beneath our feet in answer to our call, begins to rotate. As the decree momentum builds, the pulsation intensifies and the flame begins to spin.

See yourself enveloped in the violet flame. See the violet flame passing up through your physical body, caressing the body internally and externally, healing the organs, transmuting the causes of disease within those organs, reversing negative spirals of degeneration and restoring positive spirals of regeneration.

---

**I AM the Violet Flame**

I AM the Violet Flame
    In action in me now
I AM the Violet Flame
    To Light alone I bow
I AM the Violet Flame
    In mighty cosmic power
I AM the Light of God
    Shining every hour
I AM the Violet Flame
    Blazing like a sun
I AM God's sacred power
    Freeing every one

My visualization with this decree is to see a violet-flame sea of light enveloping the entire planet. I like to sing this decree to the melody of "Santa Lucia" because it evokes the action of the sea.

This is a powerful mantra. We call it a mantra because it is short and can be repeated many times, gathering momentum as it goes. It is also an I AM affirmation. Each time we say "I AM the violet flame," all of the God that is in us descends to manifest as that violet flame.

The science of the spoken Word is impersonal. Whoever calls forth the violet flame with goodwill will receive it to the blessing of himself and all life.

The science of the spoken Word is based on the geometry of

God and the mathematics of God, and it does not fail us when we do not fail it. The more we pour the fire of our being into our decrees, the more God pours his violet flame into us.

---

*To find out more about the violet flame and its uses, see the following books by Elizabeth Clare Prophet:*

Violet Flame to Heal Body, Mind and Soul

Violet Flame: Alchemy for Personal Change

The Science of the Spoken Word

# A Psalm of Life

BY HENRY WADSWORTH LONGFELLOW

Tell me not, in mournful numbers,
  Life is but an empty dream!
For the soul is dead that slumbers,
  And things are not what they seem.

Life is real! Life is earnest!
  And the grave is not its goal;
Dust thou art, to dust returnest,
  Was not spoken of the soul.

Not enjoyment, and not sorrow,
  Is our destined end or way;
But to act, that each to-morrow
  Find us farther than to-day....

Trust no Future, howe'er pleasant!
  Let the dead Past bury its dead!
Act,—act in the living Present!
  Heart within, and God o'erhead!

Lives of great men all remind us
  We can make our lives sublime,
And, departing, leave behind us
  Footprints on the sands of time....

# Discussion Questions

1. What have you learned from these case studies about the long cycles of karma and reincarnation?
2. Do you see any common themes that emerge from the lives of these very different people?
3. Which of these stories had the biggest impact on you? Why was this individual particularly significant?
4. Do you see elements of any life stories in this book mirrored in your own life? In what way?
5. In chapter 1, Elizabeth Clare Prophet speaks of her motto, "There is no injustice anywhere in the universe." What are your thoughts about this concept after reading this book?
6. In chapter 9, we pointed out how Babe Ruth and Al Capone both had difficult origins early in life. What are your thoughts about why they took such different paths?
7. In chapter 4, Mrs. Prophet says that "El Morya selected Nin as a study for us so that we could know the folly of self-worship." Why do you think the other eight individuals might have been chosen? What is the particular lesson we can learn from each of their lives?
8. After reading these accounts, has anything changed in your outlook on your life or its challenges? Will anything in your life be different from now on?

# Notes

## Chapter 1 • Karma and Reincarnation

1. David Christie Murray, *Reincarnation: Ancient Beliefs and Modern Evidence* (1981; reprint, Bridgeport, Dorset: Prism Press, 1988), p. 17.
2. Ignatius Donnelly, *Atlantis: The Antediluvian World,* rev. ed., ed. Egerton Sykes (New York: Gramercy Publishing Company, 1949), pp. 251, 254–55.
3. Pythagoras, quoted in *Continuum: The Immortality Principle* (San Bernardino, Calif.: Franklin Press, 1978), p. 19.
4. Diogenes Laertius, *Lives of the Eminent Philosophers* 8.8.4.
5. In his *Wars of the Jews,* Josephus writes, "[The Pharisees] say that all souls are incorruptible; but that the souls of good men are only removed into other bodies—but that the souls of bad men are subject to eternal punishment." (Josephus, *The Wars of the Jews* 2.8.14, in *The Works of Josephus,* new updated ed., trans. William Whiston [Peabody, Mass.: Hendrickson Publishers, 1987])

   In *The Antiquities of the Jews,* he says, "[The Pharisees] also believe that souls have an immortal vigor in them, and that under the earth there will be rewards or punishments, according as they have lived virtuously or viciously in this life; and the latter are to be detained in an everlasting prison, but that the former shall have power to revive and live again." (Josephus, *The Antiquities of the Jews* 18.1.3, in *The Works of Josephus*)
6. Matt. 5:18.
7. Deut. 32:35; Rom. 12:19; Heb. 10:30.

---

Bible references are to the King James Version.

8. Paramahansa Yogananda, *Man's Eternal Quest* (Los Angeles: Self Realization Fellowship, 1975), p. 474.
9. Brahmacharini Usha, comp., *A Ramakrishna-Vedanta Wordbook* (Hollywood, Calif.: Vedanta Press, 1962), s.v. "karma."
10. The creation of half-human, half-animal creation survives in the race memory of the planet in the Greek legends of centaurs (creatures with the upper body of a man and the lower body and legs of a horse), satyrs, and similar creatures. Edgar Cayce spoke about these creations in his readings on Atlantis. See Edgar Evans Cayce, *Edgar Cayce on Atlantis,* ed. Hugh Lynn Cayce (New York: Warner Books, 1968), pp. 71–72.
11. Gen. 9:6.
12. Rev. 13:10.
13. Exod. 21:15, 23–25.
14. Rev. 16:7.
15. Matt. 5:17.
16. Matt. 12:36–37.
17. Matt. 7:2.
18. Matt. 7:12.
19. I Cor. 9:27.

---

### Chapter 2 • Nine Lives of Henry Ford

Opening quote: Henry Ford, interview in the *San Francisco Examiner,* August 26, 1928.

1. Edgar Cayce, (1877–1945) has been called the "sleeping prophet," the "father of holistic medicine," and the most documented psychic of the twentieth century. For more than forty years of his adult life, Cayce gave psychic readings to thousands of seekers while in an unconscious state, diagnosing illnesses and revealing lives lived in the past and prophecies yet to come.
2. Plato, *Timaeus* 25.
3. *Atman* [Sanskrit "breath," "self," "soul," "Universal Self," "supreme Spirit"] in Hinduism is the inner essence of each individual, the immortal self, the indwelling God, the supreme universal Self, absolute consciousness identical with Brahman. It is the imperishable, undecaying core of man. Most Western

scholars translate Atman as the soul. However, Atman should really be translated as Spirit, "God Self" or "divine spark."

4. Anne Jardim, *The First Henry Ford: A Study in Personality and Business Leadership* (Cambridge: The MIT Press, 1970), p. 55.
5. Robert Lacey, *Ford: The Men and the Machine* (Boston: Little, Brown, 1986), p. 95.
6. Peter Collier and David Horowitz, *The Fords: An American Epic* (New York: Summit Books, 1987), p. 89.
7. Lacey, *Ford,* p. 91.
8. Collier and Horowitz, *The Fords,* p. 78.
9. Lacey, *Ford,* p. 60.
10. Collier and Horowitz, *The Fords,* p. 100.
11. Ibid., p. 104.
12. Lacey, *Ford,* p. 58.
13. Ibid., pp. 263–64.
14. For more information on the *naim,* see the detailed descriptions of this device in Phylos the Thibetan, *A Dweller on Two Planets* (Los Angeles: Borden Publishing Company, 1940).
15. II Chron. 24:2.
16. For detailed descriptions of life in *devachan,* see *A Dweller on Two Planets.*

## Chapter 3 • Nine Lives and Another Chance

1. Peter de Rosa, *Vicars of Christ: The Dark Side of the Papacy* (New York: Crown Publishers, 1988), p. 85.
2. Ibid.
3. Herbert Thurston and Donald Attwater, *Butler's Lives of the Saints,* Complete Edition (New York: P. J. Kenedy & Sons), p. 276.
4. Laurence Bergreen, *Capone: The Man and the Era* (New York: Simon & Schuster, 1994), p. 621.
5. Ibid., p. 30.
6. Ibid., p. 35.
7. John Kobler, *The Life and World of Al Capone* (New York: Putnam, 1971), p. 26.
8. Bergreen, *Capone,* p. 105.
9. Ibid., p. 116.

10. Richard Hammer, *Playboy's Illustrated History of Organized Crime* (Chicago: Playboy Press, 1975), pp. 54–55.
11. Ibid.
12. Kobler, *Life and World of Al Capone,* pp. 209–10.
13. Ibid., p. 210.
14. Bergreen, *Capone,* p. 178.
15. Hammer, *Playboy's Illustrated History,* p. 59.
16. Kobler, *Life and World of Al Capone,* p. 229.
17. Bergreen, *Capone,* p. 183.
18. Ibid.
19. Hammer, *Playboy's Illustrated History,* p. 59.
20. Bergreen, *Capone,* p. 236.
21. Kobler, *Life and World of Al Capone,* p. 209.
22. Bergreen, *Capone,* p. 288.
23. Ibid., p. 548.

### Chapter 4 • The Diaries of a Narcissist

1. Gwyneth Cravens, "Past Present," *The Nation,* December 10, 1990.
2. Marie Bashkirtseff, *The Journal of a Young Artist,* 1860–1884, trans. Mary J. Serrano (New York: Cassell, 1889), p. 178.
3. *The Journal of Marie Bashkirtseff,* trans. with an introduction by Mathilde Blind (London: Cassell, 1891), vol. 1, p. 310.
4. Peter Collister, "Marie Bashkirtseff in Fiction: Edmond de Goncort and Mrs. Humphry Ward," *Modern Philology* 82:1, August 1984, p. 53.
5. Serrano, p. 79.
6. Ibid., p. 387.
7. Ibid., p. 82.
8. Serrano, "Translator's Preface."
9. Anaïs Nin, *A Literate Passion: Letters of Anaïs Nin and Henry Miller, 1932–1953* (New York: Harcourt Brace Jovanovich, 1987), p. x.
10. Anaïs Nin, *A Woman Speaks: The Lectures, Seminars and Interviews of Anaïs Nin* (New York: Penguin, 1992), p. 64.

11. Telephone interview with Gunther Stuhlmann, October 7, 1992.
12. Nin, *A Literate Passion,* p. x.
13. Nancy Scholar, *Anaïs Nin* (Boston: Twayne Publishers, 1984), p. 9.
14. Nin, *A Woman Speaks,* p. 161.
15. Ibid., pp. 4–5.
16. Scholar, *Anaïs Nin,* p. 4.
17. Ibid.
18. Oliver Evans, *Anaïs Nin* (Carbondale, Ill.: Southern Illinois University Press, 1968), p. 197.

## Chapter 5 • The Use and Misuse of Power

1. Nathan Miller, *FDR, An Intimate History* (Garden City, N.Y.: Doubleday, 1983), p. 154.
2. On April 5, 1933, Roosevelt issued Executive Order 6102, "forbidding the hoarding of gold coin, gold bullion, and gold certificates within the continental United States." The order required all persons, businesses, and banks to deliver their gold and gold certificates to the Federal Reserve in exchange for $20.67 per ounce and made trade and possession of gold of more than $100 a criminal offense. This allowed Roosevelt to arbitrarily devalue the dollar against gold. Many economists believe that Roosevelt's New Deal policies actively delayed economic recovery by severely disrupting the dynamics of a free-market economy, which would have formed the basis for a more rapid and sound economic growth. See, for example, Jim Powell, *FDR's Folly: How Roosevelt and His New Deal Prolonged the Great Depression* (New York: Three Rivers Press, 2003).
3. Robert Nisbet, *Roosevelt and Stalin: The Failed Courtship* (Washington, D.C.: Regnery Gateway, 1988), p. 5.
4. Ibid., pp. 5–6.
5. Ibid., p. 6.
6. Ibid., p. 11.
7. Ibid.
8. Ibid., p. 60.

## Chapter 6 • Tests Passed and Karma Balanced

1. See Phylos the Thibetan, *A Dweller on Two Planets.*

## Chapter 7 • The Iron Lady

1. According to the findings of James Churchward, archaeologist and author of *The Lost Continent of Mu,* Lemuria extended from north of Hawaii three thousand miles south to Easter Island and the Fijis and was made up of three areas of land stretching more than five thousand miles from east to west. Churchward's history of the ancient Motherland is based on records inscribed on sacred tablets he claims to have discovered in India. With the help of the high priest of an Indian temple, he deciphered the tablets. During fifty years of research, he confirmed their contents in further writings, inscriptions, and legends he came upon in Southeast Asia, the Yucatan, Central America, the Pacific islands, Mexico, North America, ancient Egypt and other civilizations. He estimates that Mu was destroyed approximately twelve thousand years ago by the collapse of the gas chambers that upheld the continent.
2. Hugo Young, *The Iron Lady: A Biography of Margaret Thatcher* (New York: Farrar Straus Giroux, 1989), p. 4.
3. Spencer Warren, "The Lady's Not for Turning: The Domestic Triumphs of Margaret Thatcher," *Policy Review* Spring 1992, p. 69.
4. Ibid., p. 64.

## Chapter 8 • Charles Lindbergh

Opening quote: Charles A. Lindbergh, *Autobiography of Values* (New York: Harcourt Brace Jovanovich, 1978), p. 390.

1. Exod. 1:22.
2. Josephus, *Antiquities of the Jews,* bk. II, ch. IX:2 (Kregel Publications, 1960, 1985), p. 55.
3. Acts 7:22.
4. Scholars generally believe that these time periods in Moses' life are symbolic rather than literal. The number 40 in the Bible often describes a period of trial or initiation, as in Jesus' 40-day fast in the wilderness, the 40 years of the children of Israel wandering in the wilderness, and the 40 days and nights of rain in the Flood.

5. Exod. 2:11–12.
6. Exod. 3:2, 7, 10.
7. Abraham Lincoln, Letter to J. W. Fell, December 20, 1859.
8. *Encyclopedia Britannica* 1961, s.v. "Abraham Lincoln."
9. Interview with David Balsiger, May 19, 1984.
10. Abraham Lincoln, letter to Horace Greeley, editor of the New York *Tribune,* 1862.
11. *Appleton Cyclopedia,* 1861, p. 296.
12. Herman E. Krooss, ed., *Documentary History of Banking and Currency in the United States* (Edgemont, Pa.: Chelsea House Publishers, 1969), 2:1392–93.
13. Murray N. Rothbard, *The Mystery of Banking* (n.p.: Richardson & Snyder, 1983), p. 224.
14. David Balsiger and Charles E. Sellier, Jr., *The Lincoln Conspiracy* (Los Angeles: Schick Sunn Classic Books, 1977), pp. 58–62.
15. Elizabeth Clare Prophet, "The Abdication of America's Destiny," Part 1, *Pearls of Wisdom,* vol. 31, no. 9, February 28, 1988.
16. Phebe Ann Hanaford, *Abraham Lincoln: His Life and Public Services* (Boston: B. B. Russell, 1866), p. 168.
17. James Takach, *Lincoln's Moral Vision: The Second Inaugural Address* (Jackson, Miss.: University Press of Mississippi, 2002), p. 96.
18. Ludovic Kennedy, *The Airman and the Carpenter: The Lindbergh Kidnapping and the Framing of Richard Hauptmann* (New York: Penguin, 1986), p. 28.
19. Walter S. Ross, *The Last Hero: Charles A. Lindbergh* (New York: Harper & Row, 1968), p. 167.
20. Kennedy, *Airman and the Carpenter,* p. 34.
21. Ross, *Last Hero,* p. 149.
22. Ibid., p. 174.
23. Mark Olshaker and John E. Douglas, *The Cases That Haunt Us* (New York: Scribner, 2001), p. 170.
24. Lindbergh, *Autobiography of Values,* pp. 186–87.
25. See Robert Conquest, *The Great Terror: A Reassessment,* 40th Anniversary Edition (Oxford University Press, 2007), p. xviii.
26. Lindbergh, *Autobiography of Values,* p. 189.

27. Ross, *Last Hero,* p. 319.
28. Ibid., p. 315.
29. Ibid., p. 361.
30. Tom D. Crouch, *Charles Lindbergh: An American Life,* (Washington, D.C.: National Air and Space Museum, 1977), p. 72.
31. Ross, *Last Hero,* p. 359.
32. Lindbergh, *Autobiography of Values,* pp. 394–95.
33. Mark L. Prophet, December 14, 1969.
34. Ibid.
35. Francis B. Carpenter, *The Inner Life of Abraham Lincoln: Six Months at the White House* (Lincoln, Nebraska, University of Nebraska Press, 1995), pp. 258–59.

---

**Chapter 9 • Babe Ruth**

1. Lawrence S. Ritter, *The Babe: A Life in Pictures* (New York: Ticknor and Fields, 1988), p. 8.
2. Ibid., p. 10.
3. Robert W. Creamer, *Babe: The Legend Comes to Life* (New York: Simon and Schuster, 1974), p. 37.
4. Ritter, *The Babe,* p. 29.
5. On April 17, 1953, in Griffith Stadium, Washington, D.C., Mickey Mantle hit a baseball out of the park and into the yard of a house across the street. Legend has it that Yankees' PR Director Red Patterson had used a tape measure to find out exactly how far the baseball flew before it landed—565 feet from home plate. Thus the term "tape-measure homer" entered the lexicon of baseball.
6. Ritter, *The Babe,* p. 65
7. Leigh Montville, *The Big Bam: The Life and Times of Babe Ruth* (New York: Doubleday, 2006), p. 136.
8. Fred Lieb, *Baseball as I Have Known It* (New York: Cowar, McCann and Geoghagen, 1977) p. 158.
9. Ibid.
10. Montville, *The Big Bam,* p. 261.
11. Creamer, *Babe,* p. 351.

12. Cliff Corcoran, "99 Cool Facts about Babe Ruth," *Sports Illustrated,* July 11, 2013. Retrieved June 22, 2014.
13. Peter Kerasotis, "Home, at the Other House That Ruth Built," *New York Times,* March 10, 2014.
14. Ritter, *The Babe,* p. 137.

---

## Chapter 10 • Elizabeth Clare Prophet

1. See, for example, Sigmund Freud, *Moses and Monotheism* (London: Hogarth Press, 1939); Joseph Winsten, *Moses Meets Israel: The Origins of One God* (Boston: Rumford Press, 1999). Winsten writes: "The only known antecedent to Israelite monotheism occurred in Egypt during the Amarna Age.... The evidence that we have points inexorably to Moses as a high-born ethnic Egyptian, perhaps royal, and very likely a postulant of monotheistic Atenism, which had steadily receded from official favor after Akhenaten's death.... The Amarna Age is therefore a unique milestone in the evolution of religious philosophy.... The monotheistic belief that could not take root in its native soil lay dormant for almost a century before it reappeared as the central tenet of a mushrooming twelve-tribe entity in Asia.... Solar reference in the worship of Yahweh was widespread in northern and southern Israel, at least during the Monarchy period, and it is highly probable that the experience in Amarna was carried over directly in those Hebrews who left Egypt with Moses." (pp. 11, 12, 102, 128)
2. Harriet Beecher Stowe, *Women in Sacred History* (New York: J. B. Ford, 1874), "Martha and Mary."
3. In *Science and Health with Key to the Scriptures,* Mary Baker Eddy writes that John's vision in Revelation of a new heaven and a new earth is "indeed a foretaste of absolute Christian Science." She also speaks of "the writer's present feeble sense of Christian Science." For her, "Divine Science is the Holy Spirit, God's self-revealing and sustaining power." She drew a distinction between "Divine Science" and "Christian Science": Divine Science "had to be reduced to a form which men could comprehend [which is] Christian Science." She defined Church as that institution which demonstrates Divine Science and is designed to save the world from "sin and death." The purpose of the

Church is "to reflect in some degree the Church Universal and Triumphant," the heavenly Church.

In her memoirs, Elizabeth Clare Prophet states that Mary Baker Eddy did not commit to writing all the mysteries of God that Jesus Christ revealed to her. Some were given only to advanced students or household staff; others were committed to no one. Just before her death, Eddy told a student, "I feel I am just beginning to understand *Science and Health.*" See Mary Baker Eddy, *Science and Health with Key to the Scriptures* (Boston), pp. 573, 577; Stephen Gottschalk, *The Emergence of Christian Science in American Religious Life* (Berkeley, Calif.: University of California Press, 1973), 25, 26, 177, 36; Elizabeth Clare Prophet, *In My Own Words* (Gardiner, Mont.: Summit University Press, 2009), p. 140.

4. *St. Clare and Her Order: A Story of Seven Centuries* (London: Mills & Boon, 1912), p. 14.
5. Ibid., p. 42.
6. Raymond of Capua, *The Life of Catherine of Siena,* trans. Conleth Kearns (Wilmington, Del.: Michael Glazier, 1980), p. 106.
7. *The New Catholic Encyclopedia* (New York: McGraw-Hill, 1967), s.v. "Catherine of Siena."
8. Raymond of Capua, *Life of Catherine of Siena,* p. 116.
9. R. W. Chambers, *Thomas More* (London: Jonathan Cape, 1935), p. 343.
10. Marguerite Cunliffe-Owen, *The Martyrdom of an Empress* (London: Harper, 1900), p. 31.
11. Ibid., p. 277.
12. See Phylos the Thibetan, *A Dweller on Two Planets,* and Ernon, Rai of Suern, "Lessons Learned," *Pearls of Wisdom,* vol. 34, no. 61, November 27, 1991.
13. On August 21, 1879, the Blessed Mother with Saint Joseph on her right and Saint John the Evangelist on her left appeared in a silent visitation before the south gable wall of the small church at Knock, County Mayo, Ireland. The apparition was reportedly seen by about 18 people. Witnesses said the Blessed Mother was dressed as a queen in brilliant white raiment and wore a crown, with a rose over her forehead where the crown fitted her brow. She was gazing upward and appeared to be praying. Following this visitation, many pilgrims received miraculous cures.

### Chapter 11 • Where Do We Go from Here?

1. Joel L. Whitton and Joe Fisher, *Life Between Life: Scientific Explorations into the Void Separating One Incarnation from the Next* (New York: Warner Books, 1988), pp. 47–48.
2. *Republic* 618, 619, in Jowett, *The Dialogues of Plato*, 1:875–77.

### Chapter 12 • The Violet Flame

1. I John 1:5, 7.
2. Rev. 7:9, 10, 13–15.
3. El Morya, *The Chela and the Path* (Gardiner, Mont.: Summit University Press, 1976), ch. 6.

## A NOTE ON SOURCES

This book is based on a lecture by Elizabeth Clare Prophet delivered in Atlanta, Georgia, on October 10, 1992. A video recording of the original lecture is available from The Summit Lighthouse.

432 pp • ISBN 978-0-922729-27-2

## Reincarnation

*The Missing Link in Christianity*

by Elizabeth Clare Prophet
with Erin Lynn Prophet

This groundbreaking work makes the case that Jesus taught reincarnation. Elizabeth Clare Prophet traces the history of reincarnation in Christianity—from Jesus and early Christians through Church councils and the persecution of so-called heretics. Using the latest scholarship and evidence from the Dead Sea Scrolls and Gnostic texts, she also argues persuasively that Jesus was a mystic who taught that our destiny is to unite with the God within. Your view of Jesus—and of Christianity—will never be the same.

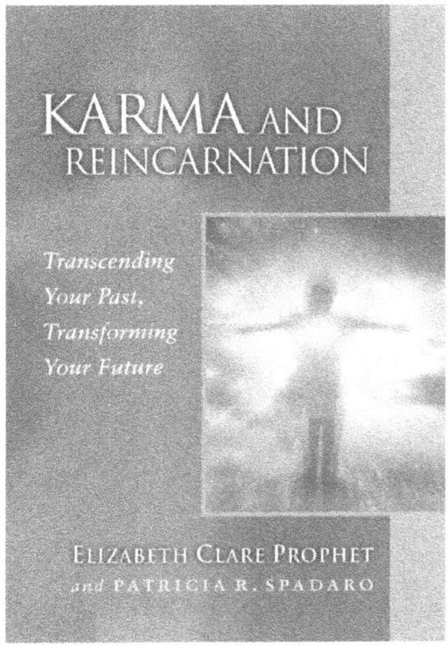


224 pp • ISBN 978-0-922729-61-6

## Karma and Reincarnation

*Transcending Your Past,*
*Transforming Your Future*

by Elizabeth Clare Prophet

The word karma has made it into the mainstream. But not everyone knows what it really means or how to deal with it. This insightful book will help you come to grips with karmic connections from past lives that have helped create the circumstances of your life today.

You'll discover how your actions in past lives—good and bad—affect which family you're born into, who you're attracted to, and why some people put you on edge. You'll learn about group karma, what we do between lives, and what the great lights of East and West, including Jesus, have to say about karma and reincarnation. Most of all, you'll find out how to turn your karmic encounters into grand opportunities to shape the future you want.

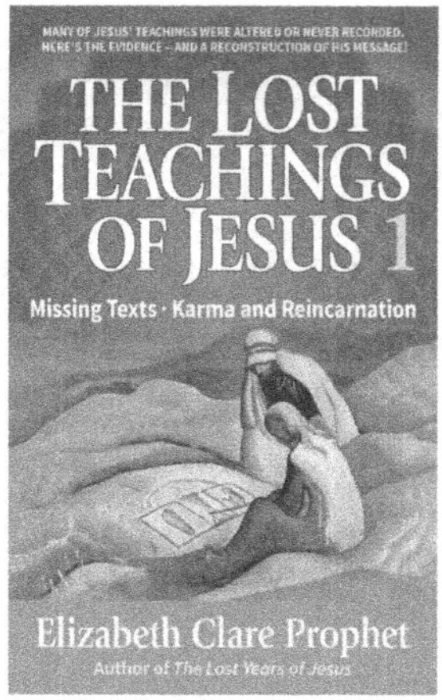


358 pp • ISBN 978-0-916766-90-0

## The Lost Teachings of Jesus 1

*Missing Texts •*
*Karma and Reincarnation*

by Elizabeth Clare Prophet

Unmistakable evidence that many of Jesus' teachings were altered, deleted or never recorded

Proves that many of Jesus' original teachings were lost, tampered with or suppressed—and that some of what was recorded is misinterpreted to this day. The author's fresh approach and penetrating insight make this compelling reading.

# About The Summit Lighthouse

The Summit Lighthouse is an internationally recognized spiritual center for the advancement of inner awakening. Our international organization is a global family that is inspired, guided, and sponsored by those known as the ascended masters.

The ascended masters are the most beloved and trusted transcendent beings guiding our planet's material and spiritual evolution. Most of the world's religions are currently based on the revelations of one or more of these masters before their ascension. We openly embrace spiritual seekers from all paths of light including the mystical traditions of the world's religions.

The ascended masters and their messengers have given us over fifteen thousand hours of invaluable inner wisdom and insightful instruction, and they have provided the means for our direct initiation into higher consciousness.

For the ascended masters . . . no subject is off limits! Their teachings contain amazing truths and awesome answers on spirituality, alchemy, astrology, sacred geometry, spiritual science, karma, reincarnation, ascension, archangels (and fallen angels), and even those issues that are considered taboo or "out of this world."

**Primary Goals of the Teachings of the Ascended Masters**

The ascended masters challenge us daily to be bold, to dare to be who we truly are, and to face adversity with courage, patience, perseverance, honesty, integrity, inner love, discipline, and discernment—all for a greater sense of inner peace, fearlessness, stillness and silence, harmony, self-mastery, compassion, and wisdom.

These teachings help our souls get back to the origin of their individualized inner source of True Self Love—the Higher Self, or I AM Presence. Our point of contact with our Higher Self is the "Spark of Life" or "Sacred Fire of the Heart," the place where our consciousness expresses its true divine nature of unconditional love and happiness, universal oneness, and an authentic desire to serve others.

### How Our Teachings Came into Being

Our teachings were all released through highly trained and trusted messengers, Mark L. Prophet and Elizabeth Clare Prophet. Mark was contacted by the ascended master El Morya at the age of eighteen and received training from him for many years before he was instructed to establish The Summit Lighthouse in 1958 in Washington, D.C.

With his ascension in 1973, Mark passed the torch for the mission to his gifted wife, Elizabeth Clare Prophet, who continued her service until her retirement in 1999.

The dictations of the ascended masters were regularly given in public. The ascended masters also inspired thousands of lectures delivered by the messengers. The content of the dictations are, by most human standards, beyond the mind's ability to construct in real time. They carry very powerful frequencies of light, awakening us to the highest truths we've ever experienced.

We leave it up to you to decide the value for yourself.

### Moving toward Your Victory

No matter what path of light you are on, spiritual freedom is attained using tools that have been passed down in wisdom teachings through the millennia: meditation, selfless service, devotional music, prayer, mantra, and the science of the spoken Word. The masters bring an accelerated understanding of these principles, especially suited for the challenges of the modern world, including dynamic decree work and the use of the violet flame.

### Next Steps

We are genuinely excited to meet you on the Path and hope you are too. We extend a warm welcome from everyone at The Summit Lighthouse, and we invite you to explore the teachings of the ascended masters at **www.SummitLighthouse.org.** Check out our free online lessons and hundreds of articles on a wide range of spiritual subjects. Browse through our online bookstore. And if you would rather talk to someone in person, please feel free to contact us today!

ELIZABETH CLARE PROPHET is a world-renowned author, spiritual teacher, and pioneer in practical spirituality. Her groundbreaking books have been published in more than thirty languages and over three million copies have been sold worldwide.

For more information about Elizabeth Clare Prophet's work, including her Pocket Guides to Practical Spirituality and her series on the Lost Teachings of Jesus and the Mystical Paths of the World's Religions, visit Summit UniversityPress.com.


The Summit Lighthouse®
63 Summit Way
Gardiner, Montana 59030 USA
1-800-245-5445 / 406-848-9500
*Se habla español.*
info@SummitUniversityPress.com
SummitLighthouse.org

Printed in the USA
CPSIA information can be obtained
at www.ICGtesting.com
JSHW051106011024
70762JS00002B/6

9 781609 884840